SECOND EDITION

EDUCATING HEARTS
and MINDS

SECOND EDITION

EDUCATING HEARTS *and* MINDS

A
COMPREHENSIVE
CHARACTER EDUCATION
FRAMEWORK

EDWARD F. DEROCHE ▪ MARY M. WILLIAMS

CORWIN PRESS, INC.
A Sage Publications Company
Thousand Oaks, California

Copyright © 2001 by Corwin Press, Inc.

For information:

Corwin Press, Inc.
A Sage Publications Company
2455 Teller Road
Thousand Oaks, California 91320
E-mail: order@corwinpress.com

Sage Publications Ltd.
6 Bonhill Street
London EC2A 4PU
United Kingdom

Sage Publications India Pvt. Ltd.
M-32 Market
Greater Kailash I
New Delhi 110 048 India

Printed in the United States of America

Library of Congress Cataloging-in-Publication Data

DeRoche, Edward F.
    Educating hearts and minds: A comprehensive character education
framework / by Edward F. DeRoche and Mary M. Williams. — 2nd ed.
        p.   cm.
    Includes bibliographical references and index.
    ISBN 0-7619-7689-2 (cloth: alk. paper)
    ISBN 0-7619-7690-6 (pbk.: alk. paper)
    1. Moral education—United States.   2. Moral education—United
States—Evaluation.   3. Moral education—Standards—United States.
    I. Williams, Mary M.   II. Title.
    LC311 .D47   2000
    370.11'4'0973—dc21   00-009508

This book is printed on acid-free paper.

01   02   03   04   05   06   07   7   6   5   4   3   2   1

Corwin Editorial Assistant: Julia Parnell
Production Editor: Nevair Kabakian
Editorial Assistant: Cindy Bear
Designer/Typesetter: Marion Warren/Lynn Miyata

Contents

Foreword

We are at one of those historic moments in public education. The American public is convinced that schooling is of primary importance and citizens across the land are deeply concerned about the quality of our schools. In the 1996 elections, pollsters repeatedly reported that our education system was the number one issue on the minds of Americans. On the other hand, shortly after the election, an NBC poll revealed that 68% of Americans award our public schools grades of C or D. We value education, but we have doubts about the instrument—our schools—that we have created to do the job.

Since the 1983 issuing of *A Nation at Risk* (National Commission on Excellence in Education, 1983), the report of President Reagan's educational commission, we have witnessed a blizzard of national educational reports citing major failings of our public schools and ending with a litany of steps and strategies for improvement. Across the nation, states have gotten the message and made major efforts to improve their public schools. Clearly, we have been and currently are in what has been variously called the "Era of School Reform," or, more recently, the "Era of School Restructuring." But regardless of what these massive efforts are called, they do not appear to be working. Data from international studies of educational achievement suggest that by global standards, our children's performance is mediocre, a fact that worries both parents and those concerned with America's capacity to compete in the global marketplace. Despite the fact that we are spending substantially more dollars and attempting a broad array of reform and restructuring strategies (e.g., decentralization, site-based management, total quality management, cooperative education, interdisciplinary learning, critical thinking,

authentic assessment, portfolios, more inclusive educational environments, year-round schooling, whole language, student-directed learning, outcome-based education, "reinvented" break-the-mold schools,
constructivism, reducing gender bias, and we are now flirting with
national academic standards), nothing seems to make more than a
short-term improvement. True reform traction does not seem to hold.

The point being made here is not that these are flawed educational approaches. Indeed, many of them are quite enlightened. In a
way, these ideas are reminiscent of the New Testament parable of the
seeds being sown in barren soil. Dedicated and energetic educators
are trying to plant fine ideas into a school environment, which has
lost its capacity to truly nurture those ideas. The "soil" of our schools
has lost a nurturing ingredient that is essential to give life to the
ideas and the efforts of educators. That missing nurturing ingredient
is the school's moral mission. By moral mission, I am not referring to
a religious creed or intention. Rather, it is the recognition by teachers, administrators, students, and their parents that they have ethical
responsibilities to one another and that, at heart, education is a
moral enterprise; that the malleable years of our children's youth are
short and crucial; that what is learned and what is not learned is
important; that what becomes habit and what does not become habit
will have great consequences for the student; and, of course, that
what one comes to believe is good and right and just will be central
to how one lives out one's life.

Somewhere in post-World War II America, our public schools
lost sight of their mission to teach our children the basic American
moral values, which have been the nation's social glue. Perhaps, as
sociologist Gerald Grant and others have suggested, the Vietnam
War and the traumas of the civil rights and countercultural revolu-
tions caused adult Americans to lose their confidence in the truth of
their moral values. In any event, it seems that over the past five
decades, we became unsure that our schools should "inculcate" or
"indoctrinate" our children with our core moral values. The fact
that, throughout history, every enduring society has been passion-
ately committed to passing on to its young its cherished values
seems to have been forgotten. Also, the inevitable fact that our children will acquire habits and moral values from their peers, from television, and from their school experiences seems to have been unrec-

ognized. In its place has been a view of schooling as a largely value-free exchange of information and skills. The teacher's role has been reduced to that of technician, one who uses various strategies to aid in the transfer or exchange of information and skills. The revered meaning of the word *teacher*, someone who helps a child mold him- or herself into something better, has been smothered in the language of competencies and techniques.

With the loss of the teacher's moral authority, comes the loss of the teacher's belief that he or she is someone who has a special obligation to each child and someone who has a call on the attention and energies of the child, there also have been losses on the part of the students. Most notable has been the loss of respect for teachers. Beyond the widespread physical and verbal abuse that teachers are subjected to is the corrosive loss of students' sense of responsibility to their education.

Where once education was seen as an opportunity to gain knowledge and to advance in the world, now it is largely taken for granted. Economists might describe education as an undervalued commodity. The fact that so many students report being bored by school is perhaps a result of their massive exposure to an enriched mediated world of entertainment. Schooling has perhaps been devalued because it is compulsory, fostering an attitude among students that service from teachers is their right rather than viewing education as a responsibility. But for whatever reason, teachers are increasingly seen by the public as unionized public servants who provide services in exchange for the taxpayers' dollars. Such attitudes and perceptions are not exactly fertile ground for a true teacher-student relationship.

No community, particularly a school community, can function long without a shared moral mission plus the language, rules, and rights that flow from it. Michael Fullan, an international expert on school reform, recently stated that the key to educational reform is the quality of the personal relationships within a school building. The connective tissue between students and teachers, adults and children, is trust or distrust, respect or disrespect, self-seeking or concern for the other. Although many of us within the educational community have lost the language of ethics and morality, it is becoming increasingly clear that this domain is central to the work of educating children.

Both university-based preservice teacher education and inservice staff development have all but ignored character education in recent decades. Other than a heavy dose of values clarification in the 1970s and a smattering of Lawrence Kohlberg's cognitive moral development in the 1980s, teachers have heard little about the moral domain. Two recent surveys, one conducted at Baylor University and the other at Boston University, provide strong evidence that character and moral education are rarely included in educator preparation programs. The same appears to be true for master's-level coursework for teachers.

What is needed most at this time is a text that merges ideas from the research on character education with a synthesis of the most effective practices in character education in schools and across school districts. Educators and concerned citizens need ready access to "what works" and a rationale for why it works. Then they can begin to include character education as a foundational element in the education of children and youth. In this volume, the authors provide a framework for a comprehensive character education program that includes leadership, expectations, school climate, implementation criteria, standards, resources, training, partnerships, teaching standard, and assessment. This framework will help educators and concerned citizens organize, implement, and assess character education programs in schools and in school districts. A unique feature of this book is the standards. There are program standards, implementation standards, curriculum standards, teaching standards, partnership standards, and assessment standards. These standards serve as the benchmarks for program development that are so needed in character education program today.

There is an emerging body of writing on character education directed at teachers and schools. A welcome entry into this literature is *Educating Hearts and Minds: A Comprehensive Character Education Framework* by Professors Edward F. DeRoche and Mary M. Williams, both of the University of San Diego. The authors, two former classroom teachers, administrators, and experienced teacher educators, have written a sound and practical book not only for educators but for anyone interested in learning exactly how schools can navigate these often shoal-filled waters. The title is unusually revealing in that it covers the book's domain so well. It is comprehensive, dealing with everything from the educational process to building partnerships, from the formal curriculum to the hidden curriculum, from consensus to assessment. It is a framework in that it places character education in historical and pedagogical perspective. And most important, the book is a practical guide to reaching both the hearts and minds of our children and helping them to develop "good characters," which is their human destiny. It is just in time.

—Kevin Ryan
Boston University

Preface

The biggest day-to-day repository of constructive power to improve schools is in the hearts, minds, and hands of people who work in them.

—Kenneth A. Sirotnik

As citizens, educators, and parents, we must insist that our children learn to become good, productive, contributing human beings. We must teach them to think rationally and behave responsibly. We must teach the love of learning, along with the love of living in a democratic society where one has rights and freedoms and, equally important, responsibilities.

To these ends, we remind you that two major purposes of schooling are cognitive-academic development and character formation. Cognitive-academic development contributes to enhancing children's and youth's knowledge and intellectual skills. Character formation helps shape their attitudes and behaviors reflected in such values as honesty, integrity, respect, responsibility, self-discipline, and care.

Cognitive-academic and character development prepare students for the world of work, for further education, for lifelong learning, and for citizenship. We will repeat many times in this book that character education programs and activities are not substitutes for, or replacements of, the cognitive-academic responsibilities of teachers and students. Rather, character education creates an environment designed to enhance the effectiveness of teaching and learning.

Our belief is that it benefits no one to have students leave school competent in the cognitive-academic aspects of their education but lacking in character.

This book, then, is about values and behaviors. It is about modeling and example. It is about community, cooperation, communication, and, above all, caring for our children and youth. All of these play out, positively or negatively, in the interactions that children and youth have in families, in peer groups, in schools and classrooms, in neighborhoods, and in the hearts, minds, and hands of the adults in their lives.

Our primary intent is for readers to use this book as a resource that will help promote character education in schools and communities. The book is written for educators, parents, and concerned citizens who wish to foster the community's consensus values among children and youth. To this end, we provide a comprehensive, practical text with a framework that includes a variety of ideas, strategies, techniques, examples, and resources for organizing, implementing, sustaining, and assessing character education programs in school districts and in each elementary, middle, and senior high school.

This is the second edition of the book. New readers will not find it necessary to be concerned about the differences in content between the first and second editions. Readers of the first edition might ask two questions: Why do I need to have a copy of this edition of the book? What is different in this edition that makes it worth reading again?

Let's examine the differences chapter by chapter. The introduction to character education in Chapter 1 offers a brief historical perspective about efforts to help students learn values in school settings. The need for character education programs is made clear with supporting evidence from both parents and public polls. The purposes of schooling and the values proposed by government, organizations, and school districts are also described.

Chapter 2 describes a comprehensive character education framework that has gone through significant changes based on commentary from educators about the framework that we offered in the first edition. The purpose of this chapter is to provide persons interested in creating character education programs in their schools and communities, or those wishing to enhance existing character education programs, with a framework that is applicable, practical, and useful in school and community settings.

"Keys" for implementing a successful character education program at a school site are outlined in Chapter 3. The content offers school personnel descriptions of nine key factors that should help in the planning and implementation of effective character education programs.

A new chapter that did not appear in the first edition is about instruction. In Chapter 4, we offer what we call the "5 C's" for each teacher's classroom: conflict resolution, classroom management, citizenship, cooperative learning, and critical thinking.

Chapter 5 is about partnerships, particularly the importance of entering into strong partnerships with parents. It is and has been our premise that schools cannot and should not "do" character education alone. Schools need partners—with parents, with the community, with youth and other service agencies, and with businesses. To help you do this, we offer suggestions and guidelines to develop long-lasting and effective partnerships.

Stakeholders and others, at some point in the process of implementing and sustaining your school's character education program, will want to know about the effectiveness of the processes being used and the "payoff" in terms of student achievement and behavior. Chapter 6 provides ideas, guidelines, questions, and principles for evaluating programs, activities, and expectations.

At the end of the book, a list of character education organizations are offered for the busy educator. The reader will note that each chapter ends with quotes, questions, and readings. We have added to each chapter information about programs under the title, "Something to Investigate." Our intent is to engage you and others in thinking about the content of each quote, to use the questions for discussion purposes, to encourage you to read the carefully selected readings, and to investigate programs that may be of special interest to you. The quotes, questions, and books should be helpful and useful for course assignments, for study groups, for professional development programs, and for council or committee members who are working to create or enhance character education programs in schools and communities.

Another feature of this book, besides the framework, is the standards that serve as the benchmarks for comparing existing programs and for initiating new programs. Standards are what makes this book different from others that you may read. As you read the chapters of this book, you will note that there are a variety of standards, including program standards, implementation standards, curriculum standards, teaching standards, partnership standards, and assessment standards.

Although there will be many examples, ideas, suggestions, and promising practices described in this book, we do not intend the book to be entirely prescriptive. Because of the differences between schools and communities, because of the varying approaches you and your colleagues may wish to take, and because of the resources available to you, we do not want to prescribe; rather, we want to propose.

The most effective character education programs are the ones that are personalized to fit the needs and interests of a school, a school district, a community, and children and youth. That means the content of this book will have to be massaged, modified, and manipulated to best meet the needs of the individual school, the school district, and the community. Our ideas need your creative interpretation as you implement them.

This book is intended for principals, teachers, and parents interested in promoting character development at the school site level. We believe the book is equally important to those educators in the school district office, the superintendent, assistant superintendents, curriculum specialists, supervisors, and, of course, school board members, local community agencies, businesses, and others who want to implement a districtwide or community character education program. This book is also recommended for teacher educators and for those studying to be teachers, administrators, and school counselors. It provides a framework for studying and debating the purposes and practices of educating, and for socializing children and youth regarding personal and civic values. It offers undergraduate and graduate students studying to be educators ideas, suggestions, strategies, and resources that will not only help them in their studies but will also help address some major school and societal problems and possible ways to solve these problems.

We encourage you to read through the entire book first, then go to any particular chapter to begin program planning, implementation, or assessment. In reviewing the manuscript, we noted extensive use of alliteration. We must confess that we had fun trying to hone our ideas and thoughts with words that begin with the same letters. We thought it a useful device for helping the reader remember key concepts and concerns.

In the first edition of this book, we asked for feedback from our readers. As we said earlier, we received that feedback and have made important changes in this edition based on our responses from teachers, administrators, and our colleagues who specialize in character education theory and practice. What we said in the first edition continues to be the case: "This book was written in response to a need expressed by people across the country for a clearly articulated plan for a comprehensive character education program." Our experiences suggest that the framework, the standards, the ideas and suggestions described in this edition will help educators create and craft successful character education initiatives in their schools and communities.

ACKNOWLEDGMENTS

Ed wishes to thank his wife, Jacqueline, who once again organized family affairs so that the research and writing for this book could be done. Special thanks to his six children who demonstrate, on a daily basis, what good character is all about.

He also wishes to thank his colleagues at the University of San Diego and the Dean of the School of Education for their support in his efforts to bring its value-based education goals and practices to K–12 schools. We dedicate this book to the University of San Diego— for the values in its mission and the character of its people.

Mary offers sincere thanks to her family, especially her husband, Richard Johnston, for listening and adding his thoughts during the process of revision. A special thanks to Kevin Ryan and Boston University for the solid foundation. Mary's work in character education has been developed further by all the national and regional association conferences that have allowed her to present and test ideas.

More thanks to her colleagues at the University of San Diego for their support. And finally, she thanks all the teachers, administrators, parents, and students who have, over the years, analyzed and critiqued her ideas and practices.

Like the first edition of this book, the second edition could not have been completed without the ideas and suggestions of those whom we read, those whom we quoted, and ideas gleaned from conversations with our colleagues. Special thanks to Erin Gross, graduate student at the University of San Diego, for both her editorial and technical assistance with this edition. We thank all of you.

We ask each reader, as you begin reading this book, to remember the words of Martin Luther King, Jr.: "I have a dream, that my four little children will one day live in a nation where they will not be judged by the color of their skin, but by the content of their *character* . . . "

Grateful acknowledgment is made for permission to reprint from the following sources.

In Chapter 1: Diegmuelier, K. (1996, February 7). AASA reform report urges focus on ethics-sidebar chart. *Education Week, 15*(20); Frymier, J., Cunningham, L., Duckett, W., Gansneder, B., Link, F., Rimmer, J., & Schulz, J. (1996). Values and the schools. *The Research Bulletin*, No. 3, pp. 3–4; Ryan, K., & Bohlin, K. (1996). *The character education manifesto.* The Boston University Center for the Advancement of Ethics and Character; and Stratton, J. (1995). *How students have changed*, p. 9. Published by American Association of School Administrators. (Copies available from AASA at 1.888.PUB.AASA.)

In Chapter 2: Fullan, M., & Miles, M. (1992). Getting reform right: What works and what doesn't. *Phi Delta Kappan, 73*(10), 749–752.

In Chapter 5: Lickona, T. (1996). *Eleven principles survey (EPS) of character education effectiveness.* New York: State University College at Cortland, The Center for the 4th and 5th Rs.

In Chapter 6: Berger, E. (1996). Locust Valley's character education program. *The Fourth and Fifth Rs: Respect and Responsibility Newsletter, 2*(2), 1–4; Leming, J. (1993). In search of effective character education. *Educational Leadership, 51*(3), 69; and Schaps, E. (1996), excerpts from a mimeograph describing the Child Development Project, Oakland, California.

The contributions of the following reviewers are gratefully acknowledged:

Barry Bashutski, Director of Education and Research
Saskatchewan School Trustees Association
Regina, Saskatchewan, Canada

Judy Butler, Assistant Professor of Secondary Education
College of Education, State University of West Georgia
Carrollton, GA

Nancy Ritsko, Assistant Professor of Counseling and Educa-
   tional Psychology
Slippery Rock University
Slippery Rock, PA

Kelly Scrivner, Director of Development
St. Clement's Episcopal Parish School
El Paso, TX

David Sidwell, Director of Theatre Education
Department of Theatre Arts, Utah State University
Logan, UT

About the Authors

*E*dward F. DeRoche received a BS degree from the University of Maine, an MEd degree from Eastern Connecticut State University, and an MA and PhD from the University of Connecticut. He is currently Professor in the School of Education and Codirector of the International Center for Character Education at the University of San Diego.

He has been an elementary and middle school teacher and principal, a public school board member, a member of two private high school boards, and a school of education dean.

Dr. DeRoche has been an officer in many state and national professional organizations. He is a nationally known consultant and researcher on using newspapers in schools. He writes a bimonthly column, "What Research Says to the NIE Manager" for *Newspaper in Education Information Services* (New York).

He is a consultant, evaluator, author, teacher trainer, and a recipient of several awards. He has published eight books and over 50 articles on educational topics. Among his most recent books are *How School Administrators Solve Problems* (1985); *An Administrator's Guide for Evaluating Programs and Personnel* (1987); *Complete Public Speaking Handbook for School Administrators* (1988), which includes speeches on moral development and character education; and *The Newspaper: A Reference Book for Teachers and Librarians* (1991).

He published a booklet on character education titled *Character Matters: Using Newspapers to Teach Character* (1999, USETHENEWS Foundation). His current articles include "Character Education Comes to California: Implications for Teachers Educators," *Issues in Teacher Education* (1997); "Character Education: A One-Act Play,"

Action in Teacher Education (1999); and "Leadership for Character Education Programs," *Journal of Humanistic Education and Development* (in press).

*M*ary M. Williams received her BS degree in elementary education from the State University of New York (SUNY), Plattsburgh, her MS in reading from SUNY, Albany, and her EdD in Educational Leadership: Curriculum, Instruction, and Supervision from Boston University. She has been a K-12 teacher, a reading specialist, a curriculum coordinator, a teacher educator, a staff developer, and a program evaluator.

She was Associate Professor at Pace University in New York and is now Professor of Education at the University of San Diego, where she is also the Cofounder and Codirector of the International Center for Character Education. She is Cochair of ATE's National Commission on Character Education.

Dr. Williams conducts regional and national workshops, hosts international conferences and academies, and makes presentations on character development, ethical issues and leadership in education, case-based pedagogy, literacy, diversity issues, technology, and authentic assessment.

Dr. Williams is author of numerous publications, including an article, "Actions Speak Louder Than Words: How Students View Character Education" in *Educational Leadership* (1993), and "A Framework for Teaching Values and Ethics," that appeared in three different language versions of *Education International* (June, 2000), and a book, *Character Education: The Foundation of Teacher Education*, the Report of the National Commission on Character Education (1999, Character Education Partnership).

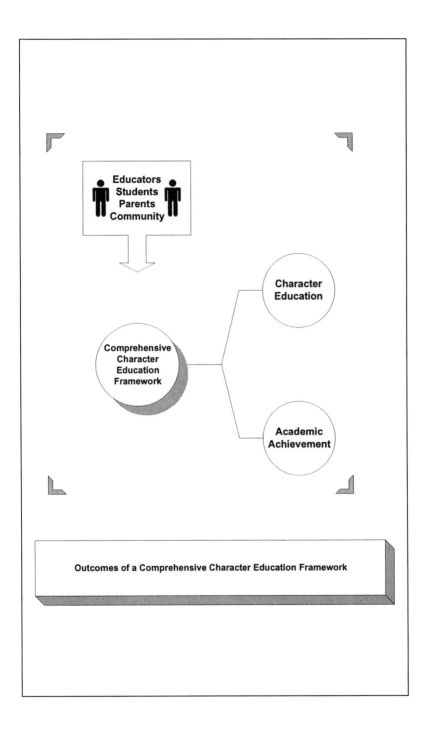

Educators
Students
Parents
Community

Character
Education

Comprehensive
Character
Education
Framework

Academic
Achievement

Outcomes of a Comprehensive Character Education Framework

CHAPTER 1

‿◦◦◦‿

Setting the Stage
for Character Education

How do you teach people to be good? What is the
point of knowing good, if you don't keep trying to
become a good person?

—Robert Coles

One of America's most respected analysts of public opinion and social trends, Daniel Yankelovich (1995), identifies three destructive trends that are causing the American public to be pessimistic, cynical, angry, and frustrated. They are the failure of most people to benefit from economic growth, the "disconnect" between leaders and citizens, and the weakening of common core values that Americans share. What Yankelovich has to say about the need for communities to come together to foster the moral and character development of their children and youth is important to those interested in participating in the character education "reformation." He states that moral confusion is widespread and that the shared norms that hold our society together are breaking down. He reports that 9 out of 10 Americans believe "the nation's social morality to be in a state of decline and decay." He claims that the core value of "individual responsibility" has eroded because "Americans today give

1

more attention to their rights than to their obligations and responsibilities" (p. 6).

If the public feels that there is a state of moral decline, "should we teach the young, in home and school, that some ways of behaving are really right and others are really wrong, or should we teach that what is right and wrong depends on what we as individuals believe" (Delattre & Russell, 1993, p. 24)? Is it inappropriate for a community to try to educate its young that there is a difference between love and hate, between good and bad, between honesty and dishonesty, between caring and selfishness? Should a community, and particularly educators, remain silent when some of the media, rock stars, professional athletes, movie stars, and political leaders promote ways of life that are contrary to moral and ethical principles (Jarvis, 1993)? We say "No!" We, like you, believe that in a democratic society there are commonly held values that children and youth need to learn. By working together with families and community groups, we can identify these values, teach them, model them, and encourage young people to practice them.

The public feels there is a state of moral decline because they have witnessed well-documented "snapshots" over the past two decades of a range of social ills, including dysfunctional families, drug use and abuse, irresponsible sexual behavior, out of wedlock pregnancies, sexually transmitted diseases, high school dropouts, family violence, in-school violence, child abuse, juvenile deaths from suicide and homicide, an emphasis on sex and violence on television and in the movies, music with distasteful lyrics, the rise of vandalism, stealing, cheating, the apparent lack of role models (a confusion between heroes and celebrities), and a general sense that many of our youth have lost qualities of civility, respect, and responsibility (to say nothing about adults who lack these traits).

It is interesting to note what the 1994 Superintendents of the Year have identified as the major changes they have observed among young people today. Their list is instructive, and it captures the public's concern (and probably youth's as well) about the state of growing up in the U.S. today. Their observations set the stage for a reformation in moral education and the banner that will carry it— character education. The 10 major changes that they identified (in Stratton, 1995, p. 9) are these:

1. The number of dysfunctional families has grown.

2. High technology has influenced school, work, and home life.

3. Children are threatened by crime, violence, ignorance, and poverty.

4. Communities are changing, becoming more diverse.

5. Mass media grips our children, giving them more knowledge at an earlier age.

6. Students question authority and shun traditional values and responsibilities.

7. A hurry-up society often lacks a sense of community.

8. Changing workplaces create demands for higher levels of literacy.

9. Knowledge about learning styles demands new kinds of education.

10. Peers exert a powerful influence on values.

There are other reasons for the public, and its communities and schools, to react to the "moral crisis," in the U.S. and to try to recapture interest in character education. Two come from a report by the National School Boards Association (1987). The first has to do with immigration, legal and illegal, which has doubled since 1950. "Immigration trends are focusing attention on the need to ensure the teaching and transmitting of a common set of shared values necessary for continuity and stability of the American culture" (p. 5). The second addresses this country's youth:

> Today's adolescents . . . are more materialistic, less realistic and/or harder to motivate than earlier generations, and that with parents taking a less active role in raising their children, youth look elsewhere for some sort of structure in their lives or suffer various problems for want of such structure. (p. 5)

Another reason for communities and schools to become involved in the character formation of children and youth is the public's call for action. Editors and columnists are warning us of the dangers of our cultural condition. Book writers are telling us that "values matter most" and that we must campaign for "moral literacy." The public has voiced concerns about crime; violence in the schools, in the streets, and in the media; the lack of discipline in schools; the loss of civility; and the need to emphasize the democratic values explicit in our diverse cultural heritage and traditions.

THE PUBLIC AND POLLS

These social and cultural concerns are underscored in public opinion polls that call for schools to help foster personal and civic values. The Phi Delta Kappa (PDK)/Gallup polls over the past two decades have shown that the public strongly supports character or moral education in the public schools.

The 1993 PDK/Gallup poll asked whether respondents thought the community could agree on a basic set of values, such as honesty and patriotism, that could be taught in the public schools. The results showed that 69% of the respondents and 73% of parents with children in schools, both public and nonpublic, thought it was possible. More than 70% of the respondents believed that schools should teach children and youth acceptance of people who hold different religious beliefs, and who hold unpopular or controversial political or social views (Elam, Rose, & Gallup, 1993).

In the 1995 PDK/Gallup poll, personal and civic values were identified and respondents were "practically unanimous" in their opinion about which values should be taught in the public schools—respect for others, industry or hard work, persistence or the ability to follow through, fairness in dealing with others, civility/politeness, self-esteem, and high expectations for oneself (Elam & Rose, 1995).

According to a 1994 public opinion poll, schools should be teaching values, with particular emphasis on tolerance and equality. "A goal for the next generation," say the authors of this report, is the "teaching of 'respect' for others and rejecting more contentious messages." This suggests that the public is "longing for harmony and civility and some desire to put discord in the past" (Johnson & Immerwahr, 1994, p. 24). In a recent study addressing what Californians want from their public schools, eight focus groups agreed that schools should assume the responsibility to teach values and highlighted the values of honesty, integrity, and respect for others (California Public Education Partnership, 1996).

Core values are common among diverse populations. Poplin and Weeres (1992) report that their findings suggest that although cultural differences, ethnic differences, and socioeconomic differences do exist in the expression and prioritization of values for people in the public schools, they still "value and desire education, honesty, integrity, beauty, care, justice, truth, courage, and meaningful hard work" (p. 14). The authors also report that students want meaningful conversations with adults and with their peers about important issues and values. The 1996 MetLife survey supports student interest in values. This survey found that public school students feel that values are an important aspect of school life and should be taught along with the principles of right and wrong (Leitman, 1996).

It is apparent through polls, through leaders, and through organizations that the public wants the schools to actively engage students in value formation and character development. It is also apparent that school personnel, parents, and especially students support school and community efforts to foster consensus values and to implement character education programs.

The social malaise that we are experiencing calls for a reexamination of what schools and the community (especially the media) are teaching our children and young people about life and living. One of the purposes of this book, and probably one of the reasons you have taken your time to read it, is to encourage action in the character formation of children and youth. We, like you, believe that life is based on moral principles and moral reasoning; that in this nation there are commonly held personal and civic values; that children and youth (and some adults) need to be educated about and practice these commonly held values; and that educators in each community should not be moral bystanders but should take leadership roles in helping parents and the community to foster consensus values. But is character education just another educational fad whose time has come and will disappear from the educational scene in a few years? Haven't we been down this values/moral development road before?

WHATEVER HAPPENED TO . . . ?

A cursory review of the past four decades may add insight into the current character education movement. We will take a look at the past four decades and then focus on "values clarification" and "cognitive moral reasoning" to discover if there are any lessons to be learned.[1]

The Fifties

A decade described as "commies, containment, and cold war," the fifties was a time of the Truman Doctrine, the Korean War, McCarthyism, and the GI Bill. Some observers labeled the decade as one of tranquility and prosperity with an abnormal fear of communism. The Supreme Court ruled on *Brown v. the Board of Education* and Eisenhower sent federal troops to Little Rock Central High School. In 1957 there was Sputnik, which led to national concern about the preparation of students in science and mathematics. This concern spurred the first major effort to provide federal aid to K–12 schools through the 1958 National Defense Education Act. The new emphasis on teaching "content" was one of the factors leading to the demise of the life adjustment education movement. Critics such as Arthur Bestor, Admiral Hyman Rickover, John Gardner, and James Conant prompted many curricular changes and one major organizational change—the comprehensive high school.

On the "values front," teachers were expected to teach traditional American values directly. *Inculcation* was an acceptable word and method, and moral education was part of the curriculum and daily life of the school with patriotic assemblies, morning prayers, citizenship recognition ceremonies, and atomic bomb protection drills. Most students respected authority, the law, and teachers. Nevertheless, under the surface, changes were taking place. There was a sense that everything was relative, situational, and personal, which was gradually moving the teachers and schools away from their traditional role as moral educators of the young.

The Sixties

Interestingly described as a decade of "years of hope, days of rage," during the sixties, the country reacted to and rebounded from the Beatles, the Berlin Wall, and the Bay of Pigs. The public's emotional strain resulted from the Cuban Missile Crisis, *Camelot*, civil rights marches, a counterculture mentality, the assassination of three of the decade's leaders, and the Vietnam War. These events also demonstrated the resiliency of the republic as it rebounded to support the Civil Rights Act and President Johnson's War on Poverty and Great Society programs. The "medium was the message," there was a man on the moon, and there was Vietnam.

On the education front, educational critics and commentators included such names as John Holt, Herbert Kohl, Jonathan Kozol, and George Dennison. Teachers and principals were introduced to programmed learning, ungraded schools, England's open education system, and a revival of Piaget's theories. There was also a rise in negative student behavior and teacher absenteeism. The federal government passed the 1965 Elementary and Secondary Education Act with a focus on early childhood education beginning with Head Start. Lawrence Kohlberg began publishing his work on cognitive moral reasoning. Professor Louis Raths published *Values and Teaching*, which promoted the idea of teacher as a value-neutral facilitator, helping students clarify their own values, and admonished any direct teaching of a prescribed set of values. An array of factors contributed to confusion and little consensus about a common core of values that should be taught in the public schools.

The Seventies

The media's headlines and stories described the public's moral confusion and cynical attitudes. There was Mai-Lai, the POWs, Kent State, Cambodia, and troop withdrawal from Vietnam. The news highlighted Watts and Watergate, *Roe v. Wade*, the Beatles breakup, and Elvis's death. President Nixon resigned, Ford took over, and in the country's bicentennial year, a new president was elected. Eighteen-year-olds got the vote, hostages in Iran contributed to Carter losing the presidential election, and the public wondered about Three Mile Island. It was a decade of distrust of the government, authority, and anyone over 30. Individual rights reigned. New sexual mores were established. Congress banned discrimination against handicapped people.

At school, educators coped with desegregation problems and busing issues, and reeled from the works of critics such as Ivan Illich (*Deschooling Society*), Charles Silverman (*Crisis in the Classroom*), Neil Postman and Charles Weingartner (*Teaching as a Subversive Activity*), and William Glasser (*Schools Without Failure*). "Open education" lost favor to a "back to the basics" movement. Many teachers seemed drained by students' and society's behaviors and focused less on moral matters and more on being dispensers of information and proponents of minimum-competency tasks and tests. Student behavior in the classroom seemed to be negotiated by some teachers and students as, "You don't bother me, I won't make you do school stuff." Teachers seemed to be merely technicians, and some publishers tried to introduce teacher-proof instructional materials. Professors Simon, Howe, and Kirschenbaum published a new book that became the favorite of educators: *Values Clarification: A Handbook of Practical Strategies for Teachers and Students*. Of the 40 books published during the decade on values clarification, this one sold an unprecedented 600,000 copies, which attested to the popularity of the movement (Kirschenbaum, 1992).

The Eighties

During the first year of the decade, the public found itself with an actor as president and a popular singer-songwriter murdered on a street in New York City. The public also learned about a new virus, AIDS, and about the "greenhouse effect." Single-parent families jumped to more than 27% of households with children, and the Moral Majority declared itself. The public loved ET, discovered PCs, and cried over the Challenger explosion and the Alaskan oil spill.

The Olympics raised national spirits, which were quickly dashed by the October 1987 stock market crash. High school students discovered that the Supreme Court proclaimed censorship of student newspapers by school officials to be legal. Teachers were introduced to cooperative learning and administrators to restructuring. School-business partnerships began to take hold. National reports pointed to a crisis in the schools and the nation's inability to compete in world markets (NCEA, 1983). A plea went out to do something about this education crisis. That something was captured in words such as *school choice, vouchers, standards, testing, privatization, core courses,* and *teacher preparation.* The public continued to express its interest in moral education throughout the decade.

Kohlberg (1981) published a book on the philosophy and psychology of cognitive moral development. His theory was that regardless of race or culture, people progress in their thinking about moral dilemmas through six stages of moral reasoning. Meanwhile, two politician-educators, one in California and the other in the nation's capital, reintroduced the word *character* to the public, affirming that character formation, socialization, and the teaching of traditional American values was a proper role for schools.

Did we learn any lessons about using schools to clarify values and foster moral reasoning?

THE NINETIES: LESSONS LEARNED

Both values clarification and cognitive moral reasoning made contributions to the character education efforts of the 1990s. Each has its proponents and critics. Both are worth examining for lessons to be learned regarding character education programs.

As you will recall, Kohlberg (1981) theorized that one progresses through six levels of moral development as one thinks about, analyzes, and discusses specific moral dilemmas. In Kohlberg's view, the teacher's role is similar to that of Socrates, asking "why" questions, teasing out the values statements that students make about the moral dilemmas presented to them. The objective of this approach is to help students be less "self-centered" (lower stage) and more "other-centered," which involves holding a broader, more understanding view of others (middle to higher stage). Kohlberg and others who used similar approaches to try to enhance moral development of the young had their critics. Some said that the moral dilemmas used for student discussion were not age, grade, or gender appropriate. Some pointed out that the program required little study of basic values and virtues that would serve as the "anchor" for students as they discussed the moral dilemmas. Still others said that these approaches were merely cognitive exercises without application to the students' world and that they did not sound a call for students to take action. Others demonstrated that the moral dilemmas on which the theories were based were not a good "curriculum fit" and were not "teacher friendly," particularly when teachers expressed difficulty knowing when a student had progressed from one stage of moral reasoning to the next. Cognitive moral reasoning did not permeate the preservice and inservice teacher training programs. Some critics suggested that the theories and research findings were gender biased, relativistic, situational, and morally neutral (Kilpatrick, 1992). Nevertheless, Kohlberg did alert educators and others to the notion that the young are moral thinkers and that discussing moral dilemmas in classrooms under the guidance of a teacher, acting as a questioner and facilitator, takes students beyond merely their own opinions and possibly enhances their moral reasoning abilities to a more mature level (i.e., stages of moral development). (For an introduction to his moral development views, see Kohlberg, 1976.)

Values clarification was much more popular than the cognitive moral reasoning approach for three basic reasons—the strategies could be used in the school curriculum, teachers felt more comfortable with it (it was less theoretical), and it had applicability to the issues of the school and the community (values could be clarified using issues of the day). But values clarification faded in the late 1980s. According to Kirschenbaum (1992), the major reason for the decline of the movement was the failure to deepen theory, expand the research, develop the curriculum, and improve teacher training. He also points out that values clarification was used and abused by many teachers. Another weakness in the values clarification approach was the premise that values clarification, by itself, would contribute positively to the moral behavior of students.

As a principal, one of the authors witnessed a teacher describing to other faculty in the teacher's lounge that she had 30 minutes left that day, so she gathered the students into a circle and had them "clarify a value" by asking them, "How do you feel about our hot lunch program?" She pointed out that before she could record their feelings, the bell rang, leaving both her and her students frustrated. She assured the teachers who were listening to her "value clarification" story that the students didn't like it and that the administration should do something about it.

The teacher's role in value clarification strategies was to be value free. Teachers were neutral facilitators, probing students with questions as they sat around, in our opinion, pooling their ignorance. Philip Vincent (1996a) notes that among the serious problems with values clarification methodology are that it promotes relativism that sends a message to the students that individuals determine what is right for them, that it emphasizes conformity rather than development, that the approach assumes students have the ability to discuss and decide without reference to criteria for making judgments, and that there is no research that helps students to think or reason morally. Again, Lickona's (1991) view is that values clarification "took the shallow moral relativism loose in the land and brought it into the schools . . . failing to address the crucial question, are the values exposed by students worthwhile?" (pp. 11, 239). Kirschenbaum (1992) gets the last word regarding the contribution that values clarification makes to character education: "It legitimized value-laden and moral issues as appropriate for schools and other educational settings" (p. 774). What is missing from both these movements is the behavioral domain—the one that governs what people "do." Character education, predominant in the nineties, merges both the cognitive and the affective approaches and adds the behavioral dimension. Character education in the nineties was more holistic. It has been defined very simply by Lickona (1991) as "knowing the good, loving the good, and doing the good" (p. 51). Ryan and Bohlin (1996) suggest that character education is a developmental process that requires knowledge, effort, and practice along with support, example, and encouragement.

So, here we are at the beginning of the 21st century with lessons learned, problems to solve, and character education beginning to take hold because the public has come to appreciate the importance of the young learning about human achievements, ethical principles, and the moral values that underpin democratic, civilized life. And it may be that in an attempt to distance itself from the approaches of the past few decades, the public has readily accepted the terms *character education* and *character development*. These terms have reintroduced one important aspect of moral development, one that is more palatable to the public, namely, socialization—helping the young learn how to live cooperatively, caringly, and civilly (Ryan, 1986).

FAD OR FASHION?

Like all of us, children today are raised in a family, influenced by their friends in their neighborhood and school, conditioned by the nature of the community that now includes television, computers, and the Internet. Given the multiple influences on children's lives and behavior, moral and character development are more than ever both a parental and a public responsibility. We recognize now, more clearly than before, that community involvement is essential. From the media to the malls, from classrooms to boardrooms, from leaders to followers, the community must take responsibility and action for meeting the needs of children and young people. We do not need scientific surveys to tell us what our own eyes and ears are revealing. History shows that when Americans have problems with their children and youth, they look to the schools for solutions. Character education is one area where school leaders must insist that schools cannot and should not be expected to do it alone.

Also, Americans look for short-term, simple solutions to complex problems. We are a public in search of panaceas and education has had its share. You may remember such fads as programmed learning, teacher-proof instructional materials, open education, ungraded classrooms, mastery learning, values clarification, minimum-competency testing, the new math, the new science, and of course, the continual swings for the best way to teach children to read. Today, whether it be fad or fashion, we are promoting cooperative learning, collaboration, technology education, service learning, partnerships, inclusion, restructuring, teacher empowerment, accountability, standards, alternative assessment, and a return to phonics, spelling, and grammar to "balance" the whole-language approach to the teaching of reading.

Will character education have staying power in P–12 schools in 2000 and beyond? The answer is yes for these reasons. First, our best, and maybe only, opportunity for children and youth to learn prosocial and civic values is between preschool and high school graduation. Second, the swelling support for character education is not only a grassroots movement, as seen in public polls, but it is also endorsed by major educational associations, by many nonprofit foundations and organizations, and by political leaders. A few examples are illustrative:

- In 1987, the National School Boards Association implemented a project for its more than 15,000 local school board members to enhance character education in the schools.

- In March 1992, the Association for Supervision and Curriculum Development, Princeton Project 55, and the Johnson Foundation cosponsored a conference at "Wingspread" in Racine, Wisconsin, to give priority to character education activities across the country. Following this conference, the Josephson Institute of Ethics sponsored a July meeting in Aspen, Colorado, at which 30 national leaders developed a common set of values designed to transcend cultural, political, economic, and religious lines. The group agreed to promote the common set of values through greater involvement with children and youth.

- In 1993, following the recommendations from the "Wingspread" group, the Character Education Partnership was formed. This national, nonprofit, nonpartisan coalition's main purpose is dedicated to developing good character and civic virtue in young people. Later in 1993, the Josephson Institute of Ethics, following the recommendations of the Aspen group, established The Character Counts! Coalition. The coalition gathered support from business, political, educational, and religious leaders to foster the common set of values that they agreed on, called the "Six Pillars of Character"—trustworthiness, responsibility, caring, respect for others, fairness, and citizenship.

Political leadership at the federal level is also a supportive factor. President Clinton, in his State of the Union address on January 23, 1996, stated "I challenge all our schools to teach character education, to teach good values and good citizenship." His call was repeated through 1999.

Secretary of Education Richard W. Riley, in his letter to superintendents of public schools providing guidance on teaching religion in the schools, had this to say about the teaching of values:

> Though schools must be neutral with respect to religion, they may play an active role with respect to teaching civic values and virtues, and the moral code that holds us together as a community. The fact that some of these values are held also by religions does not make it unlawful to teach them in schools. (U.S. Department of Education, 1995, p. 5)

Among other initiatives 1994 through 1999 were annual White House–sponsored conferences on "Character-Building for a Civil and Democratic Society." In 1995, the U.S. Department of Education supported character education planning grants in four states—California, Iowa, New Mexico, and Utah. By 1999, 30 state grants had been awarded. Another example of the federal government's interest in this topic occurred when The Character Counts! Coalition received congressional support with the passage of a bill declaring a week in October as National Character Counts! Week.

Another piece of evidence, if you wish to call it that, to support our contention that character education is not a fad and, in fact, has been simmering under the surface of education for the past three decades, is the number of school districts and schools implementing character education programs and the increasing numbers of educators theorizing and researching the topic and publishing their views and findings. Two examples make the point.

In 1996, Phi Delta Kappa International established the League of Values-Driven Schools. The league was created to foster the development of positive beliefs among students, educators, and parents. The league has invited schools to become participants in promoting the values of learning, honesty, cooperation, service to others, freedom, responsibility, and civility. PDK's efforts focus on high schools and involve all interested chapters of the organization.

Also in 1996, major players in the character education movement signed a "Character Education Manifesto" suggesting "guiding principles" that ought to be central to education reform. In summary, these principles are as follows:

1. Education is a moral enterprise requiring a continuous and conscious effort to guide students to know and pursue what is good and what is worthwhile.

2. Parents are the primary moral educators, and schools should build partnerships with the home to foster in students personal and civic virtues such as integrity, courage, responsibility, diligence, service, and respect for the dignity of all persons.

3. Character education is about developing virtues; it is not about acquiring the right views.

4. The school principal, teachers, and all other school personnel must be educated about, embody, and reflect on the moral authority invested in them by parents and the community.

5. Character education is an integral part of school life in which the school becomes a community of virtue fostering values through modeling, teaching, expecting, celebrating, and practicing responsibility, hard work, honesty, and kindness.

6. Teachers and students draw from the moral wisdom that exists in our great stories, works of art, literature, history, and biography.

7. The sum of young people's school experiences provides much of the raw material that forges their own characters.[2]

But isn't the purpose of schools to teach children and young people basic skills, thinking skills, and social skills? Where does character education fit in?

PURPOSES OF SCHOOLS

Where in an already crowded school day with a full curriculum does the school squeeze in character education? The answer revolves around the age-old question that is continually debated—what is the purpose of schooling in this country?

There are two main purposes for educating children and youth—cognitive (academic) development and character formation, which includes both personal values and civic competencies. We realize that there are many variations on this theme. We address this question because it is central to deciding whether or not a community, a school district, or a school can and will implement a character education program. If people do not agree on purposes, they are not going to agree on the need for character education, and they are certainly not going to reach consensus on the values to be taught and learned.

There are many reasons why parents send their children to school:

- To learn the skills of learning (the basic skills of reading, writing, speaking, computing)

- To learn things (knowledge)

- To learn how to think about things

- To develop skills for further education or for the workplace

- To learn positive social and personal behavior

- To learn our history, our traditions, our values as a democratic society

- To learn how to reason, how to solve problems, how to make intelligent decisions

- To learn about health and physical well-being

᧑ To learn about aesthetics and the joy gleaned from the arts

᧑ To learn how to be productive citizens

You might add to this general list those purposes that you feel are important. John Goodlad (1994), for example, lists 12 goals for schools, including one that he identifies as "moral and ethical character," the purpose of which is to have students develop

᧑ The judgment to evaluate events and phenomena as good or evil

᧑ A commitment to truth and values; the ability to use values in determining choices

᧑ Moral integrity; an understanding of the necessity for moral conduct

᧑ A desire to strengthen the moral fabric of society (p. 51)

In a Phi Delta Kappa (Frymier et al., 1995) study of core values, 10 purposes of education emerged as a result of community meetings across the country attended by educators (45%) and noneducators (55%). In rank order, the 10 purposes are basic skills, character, motivation, intellectual, psychological, social, health, vocational, aesthetic, physical. Character was described as "the educated person who is honest, responsible, dependable, loyal, and a person of integrity" (p. 29).

We already have a civic purpose of education that has public support and little controversy about the competencies or values taught. In the California *History—Social Science Framework* (History—Social Science Curriculum Framework and Criteria Committee, 1988), for example, the authors integrate skill development with subject matter content. Many skills are applicable to a character education program:

᧑ Basic study skills—essential to acquire knowledge

᧑ Critical thinking skills—question the validity and meaning of what students hear, read, think, and believe

- ✍ Participation skills—including personal skills (express personal opinions, recognize biases and prejudices, understand people as individuals, etc.)

- ✍ Group interaction skills (setting goals, planning and taking action as a group, leadership-followership skills, etc.)

- ✍ Social and political skills (identify issues that require social action, accept social responsibilities, accept consequences of one's actions, etc.)

- ✍ Civic skills—understand what is required of citizens in a democracy (individual responsibility, control aggression, civility, ethical conduct, fair play, etc.) and understand individual responsibility for the democratic system (rights, responsibilities, freedoms, participation, etc.) (pp. 22-26)

The example above shows that the relationship between personal value formation and civic competencies is a strong one, and when both become part of the community's priority and the school's goals, they complement and reinforce one another. *Character* may be viewed as one's personal characteristics and *civic* as one's public responsibilities. The public/civic behaviors listed below are illustrative of the relationship between character education and civic education. Civic education fosters the development of such behaviors as self-discipline (self-imposed standards of behavior), respect for individual worth and human dignity, respect for differing ideas and for those who hold them, concern for the well-being of others, civic-mindedness and attention to public affairs, loyalty, patriotism, understanding of pluralism, and support for equality of opportunity and for the common good (Center for Civic Education, 1995). The distinction between character education and civic education, although clearly related, is that civic education "focuses primarily upon those aspects of character that provide a basis for the citizen's role in self-government . . . [and] those values and principles essential to democratic life" (p. 10).

The basic point we are making is that cognitive and character (personal and civic) development is what public education is all about. Both should be integrated into a school's environment, as well as its curriculum, instructional strategies, and cocurricular programs. The two reasons for educating children and youth—cognitive/academic and character development—are separated here and in other publications for emphasis and for discussion purposes.

Now ask yourself, should schools and educators be bystanders in the crucial game of character formation of our children and youth? We hope you are in agreement with us that schools should teach values and should be places where such values are modeled and fostered. But which values do we teach?

WHICH VALUES?

The quick answer is straightforward—those values on which a community can reach consensus. For purposes of discussion, let's start with two scenarios.

In this scene, the school superintendent, after discussions with the teacher leadership, the school board, and others, announces that the schools in the district will not engage in the teaching or fostering of values, that the schools are value-free and will not enter a controversy over which values to foster. Teachers are to be value-neutral if any moral issues come up in class. This would not be a hidden agenda; it would be announced publicly. We leave it to you to imagine what the public reaction would be.

In this next scene, the school leadership meets with community leaders and informs them that education is a moral enterprise and that educators have a responsibility for transmitting the values held by the society in general and the community in particular. They seek community leadership assistance in educating the public about the schools' role in character development and want support in creating community focus groups to study the topic and to reach consensus on the values to be taught. The issue in this scenario is not whether schools should foster values but which values should become part of school learning and life.

There is much support for the second scenario. Currently, more than half of the states have legislation that authorizes the public schools to teach values. There are many schools and organizations that have programs that can serve as models for others. There are values that have been identified so that a community doesn't have to start from scratch. Let's examine a few examples to make the point.

The study by Phi Delta Kappa (Frymier et al., 1996) is a good place to start. In comparing values today with those 60 years ago, the researchers found that the values educators thought young people should learn, then and now, were very similar:

Right to Teach/Learn	Wrong to Teach/Learn
Democracy	Authoritarianism
Honesty	Dishonesty
Responsibility	Irresponsibility
Freedom of speech	Restricting freedom of speech
Courtesy	Discourtesy
Tolerance	Intolerance
Freedom of worship	Restricting freedom of worship
Respecting the law	Violating the law
Integrating schools	Segregating schools

Among other findings, the Phi Delta Kappa Study of Core Values committee reports that both educators and noneducators agree that

- "The home is the primary agency for developing values in the young, but school and church both have an important role to play."

- The increase in crime is primarily the fault of the home.

- Adolescents' values, although certainly not perfect, are better than teachers think they are.

- There are major differences between what educators say are the actual values being taught in schools and what should be taught.

- "Schools are not doing nearly as well in teaching values as most of the educators who responded thought they should be doing." (Frymier et al., 1996, pp. 4-5).

Now let us look at examples of state, district, organization, and individual efforts to identify the core values that should be taught in the schools. These examples, along with other suggestions in this chapter, serve to bolster the legitimacy of educators and schools playing an active role in the character development of children and youth. These and other sources have been used by educators and community leaders to convince their public and certain concerned groups that there is precedent for schools to engage in the character formation of children and youth.

States such as California, Michigan, New Jersey, Georgia, South Carolina, and Washington have education codes or resolutions that underscore the need for, the legality of, and the specific core values for character education programs in schools.

California Education Code—Section 44790
The Legislature finds and declares that there is a compelling need to promote the development and implementation of effective educational programs in ethics and civic values in California schools in kindergarten and grades 1 to 12. . . .

There is mounting evidence that well-considered programs . . . can be effective in fostering the development of ethical behavior, civic competence, and responsibility.

Basic and shared ethical and civic values include, but are not limited to, all of the following:

(A)   Human individuality, dignity, and worth
(B)   Fairness and equity
(C)   Honesty, including basic truth telling and keeping commitments
(D)   Courage
(E)   Freedom and autonomy
(F)   Personal and social responsibility
(G)   Community and the common good
(H)   Justice
(I)   Equality of opportunity

New Jersey's 1992 Senate Resolution No. 13 and Assembly No. 298
Be it resolved that every school board in the state implements
programs for the development of character and values in students
and makes the incorporation of these programs into the curriculum
a matter of the highest priority. The Assembly bill directs the
Department of Education to assist local school districts to include
character education in existing school curricula. As used in the bill,
"character education" means programs intended to foster the devel-
opment in each child of a commitment to our society's common core
values. Although each community would identify the values to be
taught in its program, these values might include compassion, cour-
tesy, honesty, integrity, responsibility, self-discipline, self-respect,
and tolerance.

Washington's Basic Education Act—Code 28A.150.210–211
The legislature intends that local communities have the respon-
sibility for determining how these values and character traits are
learned as determined by consensus at the local level. These values
and traits include the importance of

1. Honesty, integrity, and trust
2. Respect for self and others
3. Responsibility for personal actions and commitments
4. Self-discipline and moderation
5. Diligence and a positive work ethic
6. Respect for law and authority
7. Healthy and positive behavior
8. Family as the basis of society

Under a 4-year grant from the U.S. Department of Education, Maryland's State Department of Education has created a character education office. Since that time, many other states have established a character education office at the state level.

Some school districts and/or individual schools have adapted or modified "values lists" recommended by organizations or individuals. A few examples of each may be helpful. For the school district, we have selected one of the more experienced and publicly recognized school districts in the character education business—the Baltimore (Maryland) County Public Schools (Task Force on Values and Ethical Behavior, 1991). Their character education program is built from 24 core values culled from the Constitution and the Bill of Rights that are infused throughout the K through 12 curriculum. The 24 core values are compassion, courtesy, critical inquiry, due process, equality of opportunity, freedom of thought and action, honesty, human worth and dignity, integrity, justice, knowledge, loyalty, objectivity, order, patriotism, rational consent, reasoned argument, responsibility, respect for other's rights, responsible citizenship, rule of law, self-respect, tolerance, and truth (p. 9).

With regard to individuals, we offer two lists. Ernest Boyer (1995) lists these values: honesty, respect, responsibility, compassion, self-discipline, perseverance, and giving (pp. 183-185). Thomas Lickona (1991) lists honesty, respect, responsibility, compassion, self-discipline, fairness, helpfulness, prudence, cooperation, and courage (pp. 43-47).

The three character education organizations we selected offer programs and services to schools. The Heartwood Ethics Curriculum's values list includes courage, loyalty, justice, respect, hope, honesty, and love. The Character Education Partnership lists the following values: caring, respect for others, responsibility, fairness, concern for the welfare of others, and honesty. The Jefferson Center for Character Education's list is called the "Six Pillars of Character" and includes trustworthiness, responsibility, caring, respect for others, fairness, and citizenship.

Two examples of educational organizations (in addition to the Phi Delta Kappa suggestions) that have values lists to offer are the Association for Supervision and Curriculum Development (ASCD) and the American Association of School Administrators (AASA). A panel on moral education for the ASCD (1988) suggests the following "skills for moral living" (p. 29):

1. Disagreeing respectfully
2. Moral problem solving
3. Choosing wisely
4. Empathy development
5. Saying no

According to the AASA, the behaviors that students will need to exhibit if they are to be successful in the new century are

1. Understanding and practicing honesty, integrity, and the Golden Rule

2. Respecting the value of effort, understanding the work ethic and the need for individual contributions and self-discipline

3. Understanding and respecting those not like you—an appreciation of diversity

4. Capability to work with others as a team member

5. Taking increased responsibility for one's actions

6. Respect for others and authority

7. Commitment to family life, personal life, and community

8. Pride in U.S. citizenship and the knowledge of individual responsibilities in a democracy

9. Willingness to civilly resolve disagreements

10. Recognition and respect for educators

11. Being excited about life; setting goals for lifelong learning (Diegmuelier, 1996)

Many of these characteristics include the civic as well as the personal character competencies we discussed earlier. All the groups and individuals identified above have laid a foundation for character education in schools and communities.

These lists, then, are illustrative of the options that you (community members and educators) have access to as you go about selecting core values and implementing character education programs. Before we conclude this first chapter, we want to provide our viewpoint about character education as a basis for the framework that will be described in the next chapter.

CHARACTER EDUCATION:
OUR VIEW

It is our belief that the family is the prime agent for the moral development of children. We also believe that because of the pressures on parents and guardians, and because of the influence the entertainment industry and peer groups have on youth behaviors, character education assistance must be provided by the community and especially by the schools. It is our view that character education efforts must ultimately be focused at the school site, in each individual school, and the clientele that each school serves.

It is our view that teachers are moral educators in institutions that are moral enterprises. As moral educators, teachers have responsibilities for transmitting the core values held sacred by a democratic society. It cannot be done subtly and haphazardly. It must be well planned, with knowledge and forethought by as many adults in the community as possible. We look at it this way—schools and community agencies should help parents provide children and youth with a moral road map or compass. The "moral compass" will help direct children and youth along a route to living a life based on moral principles. At times, some will leave the highway, taking various routes, trying new roads, testing unmarked ways, taking turnoffs. The moral road map will be highlighted by warning signs, stoplights, caution markers, and bulletin boards describing the risks when deviating from the main route. But there will always be internal and external detectors (guidance from one's conscience and from others) along the route. There will always be stations where one can stop for directions on how to get back to the "moral highway."

We believe that the moral road map is one's guide to moral literacy. Whatever list of core values a community and school district uses, it is our view that educating the public and gaining community consensus precedes implementation of a character education program in schools. In conclusion, we propose that character education

- Is a concerted effort by the community and the schools (through its mission and goals) to educate children and youth about an agreed-on set of values

- ↩ Begins in a family setting

- ↩ Occurs when children and youth witness and imitate adults and peers modeling the consensus values

- ↩ Continues in the community (churches, youth groups, etc.) and in the schools

- ↩ Occurs when children and youth come to know the values through the school environment and its curriculum and cocurricular programs

- ↩ Occurs when children and youth have opportunities to study, clarify, reflect, reason, decide, and act on the values

- ↩ Is enhanced when children and youth are provided guided and supervised opportunities to engage in and practice the values

- ↩ Is verified or modified when participants assess the extent to which the programs and activities have met their mission, goals, and expectations

- ↩ Is verified when students and adults demonstrate and model the values

CAUTIONS AND BARRIERS

We suggest that you approach the facts and findings reported in this book with some caution coupled with enthusiasm that something positive seems to occur when schools participate in character education efforts. Success rests on preparing in advance for potential barriers that may appear along the way. The cautions are as follows:

- ↩ Few controlled, comparative, or empirical studies exist; that is, there are not many studies that "control" for a number of variables nor compare students in character education programs with students of similar backgrounds who do not participate in such programs.

- ✒ Methodology in many studies does not allow for generalizability; that is, what may seem to be working in one community, school district, or school may not apply to others.

- ✒ Program development and implementation is outpacing research efforts.

- ✒ Most studies have been done at the elementary level (up to Grade 6).

- ✒ Dramatic changes in student behavior resulting from any program should not be expected because behavioral change is incremental and developmental.

Listing these cautions should not deter you or those involved in character education efforts from program development and implementation. It is clear that more research is needed and more in-depth assessments need to be made. It is obvious that a greater knowledge base is necessary before any conclusive statements can be made about the effect of character education efforts to positively influence students' behaviors in and out of school.

Does this mean that we should sit back and wait for the research to catch up with practice? Should educators and community leaders lessen their efforts to teach the young the community's consensus values? The obvious answer is no—for some very good reasons. Forgive the alliterations, but we know that climate counts, that modeling matters, that promises made may be fulfilled by programs and practices, and that participants' perceptions about the worth of character education efforts are positive.

The key to success is to answer the "why" question. The facts, findings, and feelings reported in this book illustrate that there are a variety of insights and opinions about the effect of character education programs on student behaviors, particularly on whether such programs help students learn, practice, and demonstrate prosocial behaviors and the community's consensus values. The best advice may be to "look and learn," that is, look at what others have done and learn from the things you have tried. Learn both from successes (what works) and from failures (what doesn't work).

CONCLUDING COMMENT

We hope that this chapter has served as a useful introduction to the character education framework that will be described in the next chapter. Our purpose in providing you with some background information about this topic was to offer you a perspective of the need for and importance of a character education program in your school. In addition to reviewing the transitions that have occurred in the past few decades, we also shared our views and those of specialists in the field about character education. We hope that defining the purposes of schooling, clarifying the values that underscore a school's character education program, and examining the education codes of a few states were valuable to you. As you set the stage for your school's character education program, we asked you to recognize the barriers you might face and to heed our cautions. Now that the stage is set, we offer you a framework that has been modified and improved. This framework captures all the major components of a comprehensive character education program.

QUOTES:
Something to Think About

Manners and morals have been diminished by those who claim that whatever they think or do is right if it feels good to them . . . and that efforts to restore moral instruction in the schools have been resisted by relativists who proclaim that whatever one does is right and whatever one wants is good.

—Silber, J. (1993). The problem of character education.
Boston University: School of Education Newsletter, *p. 3.*

The development of good character cannot be separated from the basic purposes of education—to lead persons out of ignorance and helplessness so that they have the chance to lead positive, purposeful, productive lives for themselves.

—Delattre, E., & Russell, W. (1993).
Schooling, moral principles, and the formation of character.
Journal of Education, 175(2), 42.

*This nation is not about race, religion, culture, ancestry, or lan-
guage. None of those things defines us. We are defined only by what
we believe a society ought to be. . . . In this decade, less is being asked
of us for the privilege of American citizenship than has ever been
asked of any generation in the history of this nation.*

—Butler, O. (1989). *The case for
comprehensive upgrading of American education.*
The Carnegie Corporation Occasional Papers, *p. 9.*

QUESTIONS:
Something to Talk About

1. What concerns you most about this society? Your community?

2. In your opinion, will character education programs be strong
   enough to modify the antisocial behavior of some children
   and youth?

3. How can you find out about your state and local school district's philosophy and policies about character education?

4. What values are important to you? Which of these values
   should be taught in the schools and in your community?

5. In your opinion, will character education be an education fad
   that may disappear in another few years?

BOOKS:
Something to Read About

Brooks, B. D., & Goble, F. (1997). *The case for character education.*
Northridge, CA: Studio 4 Productions.

Lickona, T. (1991). *Educating for character: How schools can teach respect
and responsibility.* New York: Bantam.

McClellan, B. (1999). *Moral education in America.* New York: Teachers
College Press.

Vincent, P. F. (1996). *Promising practices in character education.* Chapel
Hill, NC: Character Development Group.

PROGRAMS:
Something to Investigate

The Giraffe Project

Program: America needs people with vision and courage—people willing to stick their necks out and take responsibility for solving tough problems: from violence to hunger to pollution. The Giraffe Project has been finding these "Giraffes" since 1982 and telling their stories in the media, in schools, and from podiums—inspiring others to stick their necks out. The Giraffe Heroes Program is a story-based curriculum that teaches courageous, compassionate, and active citizenship. It also provides an engaging and effective structure for service learning and for meeting community service requirements. The program includes teaching guides that begin by telling students the stories of real-life heroes, taken from a story bank of more than 850 Giraffe Heroes. Students then look in their schools, families, and communities to find more real heroes, whose stories they bring back to school. In the final phase of the program, the students create and carry out a service project they design to address a community problem that concerns them. Giraffe Heroes training gives educators from a school or an entire community a firsthand experience with classroom materials. The Giraffe Media Service has placed Giraffes' stories on all the major television networks and in hundreds of publications. Giraffe speeches and workshops bring inspiration and street-smart strategies to communities, conventions, companies, service organizations, and government agencies. Giraffe Productions is developing television programming for families and for children, based on Giraffe stories and themes.

Results: "The curriculum underlies everything the children do the rest of the year," reports one third-grade teacher, "because it changes them into a community of learners" (NEA 1/99; www.nea.org/ neatoday). Students put what they learn about heroes' courage, compassion, and responsibility into action. The kids look around, decide what they want to change for the better, then design and carry out a project to make it happen. Making their own observations and creating a response is critical to their sense of taking personal responsibility for something beyond their own lives. When they hear stories, tell stories, and become the story, the elements of character emerge in their thoughts, feelings, and actions—out of their own experience. We see kids ending up with a sense of responsibility and self-respect that spills out all over their lives. The process helps them come upon their own compassion and experience their connection to other individuals and to their community. Students find the courage to overcome their own fears, they see their taking responsibility lead to results, and they recognize that results are good. It happens by using stories to reach straight into the heart (Medlock, 1995).

Contact: Ann Medlock, President, The Giraffe Project, P.O. Box 759, Langely, WA 98260; Tel: (360) 221-7989; Fax: (360) 221-7817.

NOTES

1. Sources for this section include Dickson (1991), Davis (1990), and Gitlin (1987).

2. These principles were made available to us through correspondence from Professor Kevin Ryan (March 1, 1996) and are also available in Ryan and Bohlin (1996).

CHAPTER 2

◌ᥬᥖᥬ◌

Framework

Standards for Planning and Implementation

> *We would need information . . . to say for sure what schools can do that "works." This does not mean that schools can or should abandon their efforts to shape the young; to say that we do not know what works is not to say that nothing works. It does mean that school people, along with parents, school boards, and students, must rely heavily on their own experience as they try to put together the bits and pieces of what we do know.*
>
> —Helen Featherstone

People across the country have been asking for a workable framework that contains a clear picture of who should be involved in character education, and how those who are involved can be best engaged in efforts for enhancing the values and prosocial behaviors of children and youth. The framework described below is easily

Figure 2.1. The Comprehensive Character Education Framework

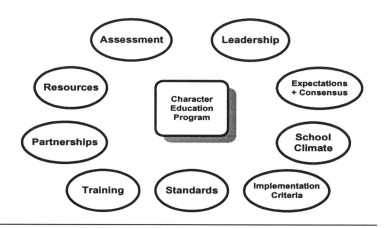

The Comprehensive Framework
Nine Keys to Success

adaptable to the three organizational patterns outlined in the latter part of this chapter.

THE FRAMEWORK FOR CHARACTER EDUCATION PROGRAMS

The framework, described in this chapter (Figure 2.1) and in Chapters 3, 4, 5, and 6, is captured in some carefully selected words: leadership, expectations, climate, implementation, standards, training, partnerships, resources, and assessment. These words are the foundation that helps focus on the concepts and ideas essential to successful character education programs. So what is our intent in offering a framework? What are the purposes of the framework?

Basic Premises for the Framework

The answers to these two questions are provided in the following premises, which are offered to help you better understand the framework's design and our intent.

- The components of the framework are the building blocks that create the foundation on which character education programs can be constructed.

- The framework serves as a blueprint or template for current or new programs.

- The framework is intended to be a template with the possibility for as many variations as there are schools that may use it.

- The framework is a reminder to stakeholders to attend to the many factors and components that comprise a comprehensive character education program.

- The framework is only one of many possible designs for character education programs.

- The framework is designed with the intention that it will be revised and modified by local educators and community leaders.

- Successful implementation of the framework will depend on the skills, talents, enthusiasm, and commitment of individuals and groups to the vision and goals of character education programs.

- The framework supports community-based efforts, which must involve creating effective relationships between and among homes, schools, and community organizations and civic groups.

- The framework is based on the premise that democratic principles and practices are, or should be, the norm in each school.

ـ๑ The framework is based on the assumption that the stakeholders have reached consensus as to which values (virtues, traits, prosocial behaviors) will be taught, learned, modeled, and practiced.

Leadership

It is not by happenstance that we place leadership as the first component of the framework. There is sufficient evidence to suggest that if there is no leadership at the school site, educational reform, school change, or new programs will diminish. Henry Huffman's (1994) experiences in creating a character education program in his community make the case for strong leadership, particularly from school administrators.

Leadership in schools appears to be shifting to one that is based on teamwork, that creates community, that requires ethical and caring behaviors, that fosters shared decision making, that enhances the growth of people, and that empowers the stakeholders in an organization.

Larry Spears (1998), CEO of The Greenleaf Center for Servant-Leadership, offers 10 characteristics of "servant-leadership" (to serve first and inspire to lead) that we feel capture the requirements to lead a school's character education program. These 10, coupled with our own interpretation of the meaning of each of the characteristics as each might apply to leading a character education program, are

1. Listening—intently and reflectively to those who support or do not support character education in the school

2. Empathy—understand, accept, and recognize the talents, weaknesses, and good intentions of coworkers

3. Healing—help heal difficult situations

4. Persuasion—building consensus about the values to be taught in the school's character education program, convincing others of its value, and making minimal use of positional authority

5. Awareness—understanding of all aspects of character education, self-understanding of the values to be fostered, and approaching situations holistically

6. Foresight—intuition, ability to foresee the potential outcome of a value-based character education program

7. Conceptualization—have a vision about and a mission for the school's character education program

8. Commitment to the growth of people—developing staff is essential; enhancing the talents and leadership roles of all stakeholders in the school's character education program

9. Stewardship—helping all stakeholders work for the greater good of the children and youth they serve

10. Building community—building a sense of community in the school so well articulated by the Child Development Project (1994) and many of the specialists in the character education field

We now wish to discuss three factors either implied or stated directly in the 10 characteristics above: vision, mission, and organization.

Vision

As you conceptualize (your vision) of the character education program in your school, we ask that you use our vision as a template for what you dream.
We envision schools

- Having high expectations for student achievement and behavior

- That are a community of learners where there are clear, consistent, coherent, and congruent messages about teaching, learning, and behaving ↄ In which students learn the values, attitudes, skills, and knowledge that they need to be successful and contributing citizens

ↄ That nurture respectful relationships, civility, trust, loyalty, care, and collaboration

ↄ Having character education programs that meet the standards described in this book

Mission

The business literature states quite convincingly that successful businesses have, among other things, a clear and purposeful mission statement. Each school should have a mission statement that captures the purposes of schooling and the elements of a character education program. Here are three examples from school districts in Missouri:

> We believe that, within the cultural diversity of schools, there is a core set of beliefs and character traits that we share. The primary emphasis of the personal responsibility program in the Kirkwood School District is to develop personal qualities in learners (birth–12th grade), so that they are assets to society.
>
> *—Kirkwood School District*

> The district's mission, through a partnership with home, business, and community, is to guarantee an exemplary educational program for students and residents that forges academically and ethically responsible citizens, prepared to live in a challenging world.
>
> *—Mehlville School District*

> The district's mission is to strive to develop in all its children the strength of character, the skills, the knowledge, and the wisdom necessary to build creative, productive lives and contribute to a global society.
>
> *—Clayton School District*

We urge you to ask yourself these questions:

- Does your school have a mission statement? If not, why not?

- What is the mission of your school?

- Is there a separate mission statement for the school's character education program, or is it incorporated into a single comprehensive mission statement?

- How effectively is the mission statement communicated within the school and to the public?

Organizational Patterns

As we have stated, we recognize that organizational patterns will vary from community to community. Our discussion will focus on the school site and the need for personnel in a school to form some kind of group to do essential tasks. We will call this group, for purposes of discussion, the school's "Character Education Council."

One question, frequently asked, is, "Who should be on the council?" Our suggestion is this: as many stakeholders as possible, but not too many to detract from the council's work. The council should have representatives from the following groups:

- School personnel (teachers and staff)

- Students

- Parents

- Community leaders

- Youth organizations

- Central office personnel

Examples of each of the three most common character education organizational patterns will be informative and helpful.

At the community level, we have selected the character education program in Duncanville, Texas. This community-based program began when the police chief rallied the community, especially community leaders, elected officials, and school district administrators, to use drug asset forfeiture funds to support a community character education program. The program's focus is on language and on STAR, developed by Dr. Brooks at the Jefferson Center for Character Education. The focus on language is based on the premise held by Dr. Brooks that "language leads to attitude and attitude leads to behavior." STAR is an acronym, promoted throughout the Duncanville community, that stands for "Success Through Accepting Responsibility" and "Stop, Think, Act, Review."

The schools and community promote STAR themes each month, such as "Be Confident," "Be Responsible," and "Be a Doer." Community involvement includes the police department, which sends one police officer to each school at least once a month to present certificates to the STAR students of the month. The school district promotes the program through a variety of activities, helps identify the STAR students, and works closely with the community to promote an end-of-school-year rally where all STAR students come together to celebrate their recognition. The chamber of commerce and businesses display STAR posters and themes of the month. They also engage in an adopt-a-school program and send personnel to the schools to talk to students. The church community shares the STAR themes in sermons, services, and publications. Civic organizations become major players in the program by reinforcing the use of the "language," and by promoting the STAR themes at their meetings and in their projects. By using the term *language*, they refer to words related to the values being taught (e.g., respect, fairness, and honesty). The local media also promote the language and themes, as well as provide coverage of school and community events, particularly the achievement-recognition rally. Parent-teacher associations help parents accept responsibility for the language and themes in homes, at meetings, and in association activities. Young adult involvement, through school and community youth groups and organizations, provide peer leadership and reinforce the language and themes at meetings and in their activities. The language and STAR themes are but one of several intervention programs in the community. The Duncanville community's involvement in character education is so extensive that its logo reads, "A Community Building Character and Responsibility: How a community with pride, teamwork, and the spirit of cooperation can work together and through language build character and responsibility."[1]

An example of the school district pattern is the character education program in the Houston Independent School District. Excerpts of three paragraphs from the district's executive summary report serve to illustrate the program.

> The Houston Independent School District is beginning the seventh year of the character education program which was unanimously approved by the Board of Education in March, 1989. . . . The plan involved contributions from the corporate and foundation communities which resulted in an unprecedented amount of financial contributions supporting the district wide implementation of a character education program.
>
> The objectives of the character education program were designed to address two global objectives: district wide implementation involving parents, community, and school personnel in the moral development of students . . . to assist teachers in understanding the values of character education as it related to student achievement and to facilitate successful implementation of character education in their classroom with skills to infuse character development into the curriculum and providing lessons specific to moral dilemmas facing students today.
>
> The initial phase of the program involved the hiring of 14 specialists and a director who developed the workshops, trained personnel, and made site visits to assist in implementation. After a 4-year period, the character education specialists were phased into positions in the Staff Development department and continue to implement the character education program as well as provide workshops in all phases of staff development as needed district-wide.[2]

As an example of a school site pattern, we have selected Antelope Trails Elementary School in Colorado Springs, Colorado. Principal Judith Casey reports that she used schoolwide discipline as a starting point in developing a citizenship program and gave attention to the affective aspects of the children's education. She outlines several specific steps that were used in creating the school's character education program.

1. Assess the Three R's of Change:
   a. Relevance—Parents and staff members stated the need for clear expectations in the area of citizenship.
   b. Readiness—Given the stated need, it seemed that the school community was ready to begin a citizenship program.
   c. Resources—The principal and counselor read many books and articles related to citizenship and character education.
2. Involvement—We felt that parents and staff members needed to be involved in program development, and so the program needed to provide ongoing opportunities for input and guidance at each step along the way.
3. Plan of Action—Parents and teachers had an opportunity to join a study committee, which involved writing a document that included a rationale, student goals, and guidelines for implementation.
4. Staff Involvement—The Character Education document was presented to the staff at an August meeting. The Teacher Advisory Team provided input and guidance throughout the school year. Staff members helped design the implementation plan that called for (a) integrating the 13 character traits into the curriculum units at each grade level, and (b) working closely with the counselor in planning grade-level lessons.
5. Communication—Parents were kept informed. All parents received a copy of the rationale and student goals and a program description was given in a parent newsletter. The Character Education Program has been well accepted by parents and staff members.[3]

Other examples of the school site pattern can be found in *Schools of Character* (1998). This booklet describes award-winning character education programs and shows how these schools organize to deliver the program and some of the highlights resulting from their organizational plan, which includes such factors as

- Staff development
- Parent involvement and support
- Monthly themes
- Weekly virtues
- Family service ideas
- Student-run assemblies
- PTA support
- Special activities and assemblies
- Peer mediation
- School and community service
- Student recognition programs
- Linking character with the curriculum
- Developing student leadership
- Creating a behavior code contract
- Working with community agencies

Once the school's council is organized and functioning, it must attend to the "heart" of any character education effort—schoolwide activities, the curriculum, and the cocurricular programs. To this end, we suggest the council use the program standards that follow.

Program Standards

The 15 program standards listed below are applicable to all three organizational patterns—community, school district, and school site. A character education program that follows these standards will provide stakeholders with adequate opportunities to gain the knowledge, attitudes, and skills to make competent, high-quality decisions about action plans for the community and schools, as well as other community organizations and agencies.

Standard 1

A comprehensive character education program is organized to support the efforts of parents or guardians in child-rearing and value formation.

Standard 2

A comprehensive character education program is implemented only when the leadership educates the public about the need for the program and helps the community reach consensus about the values to be fostered.

Standard 3

A comprehensive character education program has a coherent rationale that is reflected in the mission, goals, and expectations of the group(s) responsible for the program.

Standard 4

A comprehensive character education program provides opportunities for meaningful involvement of a wide variety of diverse community members and organizations.

Standard 5

A comprehensive character education program is organized so that its stakeholders attend to these standards and to the other components of the framework.

Standard 6

A comprehensive character education program has sufficient financial, personnel, and programmatic resources so that stakeholders can fulfill all or most of their goals and expectations.

Standard 7

A comprehensive character education program allows the school district and individual schools to take the leadership in communication, program development, implementation, and evaluation.

Standard 8

A comprehensive character education program is organized so that the stakeholders contribute to the school district's and school site's programmatic and assessment efforts.

Standard 9

A comprehensive character education program provides ongoing staff development, educating all school personnel about the need for such a program, the community's consensus values, the rationale and research, current practices, and the development of new programs or adaptation of existing programs.

Standard 10

A comprehensive character education program involves all participants in ongoing and longitudinal evaluation plans beginning with a collection of baseline data.

Standard 11

A comprehensive character education program is organized to encourage each school to develop its own program objectives, instructional strategies, activities, curricula, materials, and assessment plans in concert with the school district's and the community's vision, goals, and expectations.

Standard 12

A comprehensive character education program establishes and sustains school and community environments that foster the community's consensus values.

Standard 13

A comprehensive character education program improves the quality of school life for students, their families, and all school personnel.

Standard 14

A comprehensive character education program builds strong, long-lasting relationships between home, school, and community.

Standard 15

A comprehensive character education program contributes to the intellectual, moral, and civic literacy of students in its program(s).

The Six "P's"

There are some basic parameters for organizing a Character Education Council that need your attention.

Players

In most organizations, there are the leaders and their followers; those who actively participate and those who watch; those who support and those who criticize; and, of course, those who don't care. We are addressing those who have "signed on" to get things done because of their concern about children and youth. The council operates with representatives from each of the organizations, as described previously.

How does a school get such a council started? It usually starts through the efforts of individuals and/or groups who are concerned about the children and youth at the school. It starts with a concern, a need, a problem. Concerned individuals form groups, discuss the problems, identify needs, enlist community leaders and other stakeholders, and then an organization is created with a rationale, a purpose, and an invitation to others to become members.

The membership will vary according to the size, location, and nature of the community in which the school resides. The key point is that membership should represent as many of the stakeholders in the school's community as possible, including students, and yet not be so large that it is unable to get its work done. The school-site pattern suggests that the leadership for the character education program comes from school personnel with assistance from the community.

We made this point before and we want to underscore it here: In character education, like many school intervention programs, schools cannot do it alone. They need community help. James Leming's (1993b) comprehensive research shows that the greatest potential for changing children's behavior (which is why communities and schools are joining the character education movement) is in community-based programs that broaden the range of significant others for students. Though a school may create its own character education program, that program should be tied closely to parent and community efforts.

Processes

There are many tasks that need attention when organizing a council. As the players come together, someone has to be designated to attend to the operational needs of the group. Someone has to manage the affairs of the group, helping members set agendas, call meetings, arrange time schedules, take minutes, set meeting places, monitor the environment in which the meetings are held, and collect and distribute materials to be read for each meeting. Next, the members should be expected to discuss and answer the following organizational questions:

- ✎ Does each member know why he or she has been invited to membership on the council?

- ✎ Has the council been organized so that it can do business effectively and efficiently?

- ✎ Has a director or chair been appointed, elected, or hired?

∽ Has support staff been identified (e.g., secretarial services)?

∽ Have office space, equipment, and supplies been obtained?

∽ Have meetings been scheduled?

We recognize that implementing a comprehensive character education program is a complex and interactive process. So it may look different in each school, though these parameters look the same on paper.

Purpose

As the school council is forming, many of the implementation criteria (the "11 C's") we describe in this chapter occur, some naturally and some that require careful attention by the membership. One of the most important functions of the council is to take its time—time to let members get to know each other; time to discuss and clarify issues, concerns, problems, and possibilities; time to talk about values, to find out where each member stands on which values; and time to attend to questions such as the following:

∽ Does the council have a mission statement?

∽ Does the council plan to develop short- and long-term plans for its own work and for the character education program?

∽ Does the council have suggestions/directions for each of the organizations that are represented?

∽ Has the council attended to the criteria and standards recommended in this book?

∽ Have members been given materials to educate themselves about all aspects of character education?

∽ Do members have opportunities to attend character education seminars, courses, or conferences?

∽ Do members have opportunities to visit communities and schools that have implemented character education programs?

It may be, then, that in the first year of the school's Character Education Council, members and other stakeholders spend time discussing and clarifying efforts so that when consensus has been reached on the democratic values (both personal and civic) that are desired for the children and youth in the school, the council is ready to "go public" if it has not already done so. Only after such discussions should the group consider their readiness to implement plans, support programs, and check on progress.

Plans

After the council members have sorted out their own ways to do business and have reached consensus on the values to be promoted or fostered in the school, they need to invite, inform, and involve others, and they need to begin implementing plans and programs. The public needs to be invited to the conversation about the need for value formation in children and youth. The council needs to plan for active involvement of as many individuals and organizations who wish to participate as is possible. It needs to develop ways to help people come together for discussion and action. It needs to have the school's stakeholders reach consensus on the values to be fostered. In sum, it needs to expand the stakeholders' pool, expand the resource opportunities, and expand the plans of action. The council has to attend to a myriad of things to do, such as

- Determine how to get school-community consensus.
- Invite stakeholders to suggest practices and programs.
- Encourage innovation and flexibility in the plans that are proposed.
- Create a clearinghouse of materials on character education for the community to use.
- Involve the media.
- Make presentations to community groups.
- Create community-level conferences and seminars.
- Monitor progress toward goals and objectives.

- ๑ Set timelines.

- ๑ Arrange school information and celebration sessions.

- ๑ Focus on the needs, interests, practices, and resources at the school.

Practices

Each council will offer an array of practices—things that are to be done in the school. Our intent here is to list a few things that schools can do as examples.

1. Get media coverage of character education efforts.

2. Display the values on signs, banners, and bulletin boards.

3. Create brochures and pamphlets on each value.

4. Plan for institutionalizing the values and integrating them into the curriculum.

5. Hold fairs, create videos, display student portfolios.

6. Hold special assemblies and recognition ceremonies.

7. Involve parents and the community (see Chapter 5).

8. Create or enhance community and in-school service learning practices.

9. Coordinate the character education program with other intervention programs, such as conflict resolution, pregnancy prevention, or drug education.

10. Have teachers, individually or in teams, create their own professional development plans.

11. Coordinate school practices with other programs in the community.

12. Identify a person or team that will serve as the character education school site coordinator or community council director.

13. Develop student leadership opportunities in the classroom, school, and community.

Progress

The last of the "P's" that needs attention by the council is *progress*. This word means assessment and evaluation; that is, progress toward goals and expectations should be assessed using a variety of evaluative strategies. Tracking progress helps form future plans; tracking progress helps determine what is working and what is not; tracking progress helps determine the best allocation of resources; tracking progress keeps the community informed. We'll say no more about progress here because we devote Chapter 6 to the topic of evaluation.

Expectations: Some Questions to Guide Decision Making

We now want to provide you and others with a set of expectations in the form of questions. We pose these sample questions as a way to determine what the stakeholders want from the school's character education program. We don't have answers. You, and those who are organized to provide character education programs, will have them. These questions are tools for thinking, designed to spark discussion and to help make informed decisions. They serve as an introduction for the assessment ideas described in Chapter 6. Ten sample questions are

1. If you (organizations/councils) are going to engage in a character education program, what are your expectations?

2. What outcomes are you looking for?
   a. Better student behavior at school?
   b. Better behavior in the home or community?
   c. Fewer classroom disruptions?
   d. Evidence that students have learned and are practicing the values taught?
   e. Examples of students respecting adults and each other?
   f. More students doing their homework?
   g. More parents reporting positive behavior changes at home?
   h. Demonstrated moral literacy in the cognitive, affective, and behavioral domains (thinking, feeling, doing)?

    i. A developed and demonstrated sense of efficacy and self-respect?

    j. An understanding of multiple perspectives?

    k. Witnessing students demonstrating concerns for the welfare of others?

    l. Application of skills of moral reasoning and ethical decision making to solve problems?

    m. Demonstrated skills of social cooperation?

    n. Demonstrated responsibility by students for their own learning?

    o. More students exhibiting a positive attitude toward learning, classroom work, and school?

3. What percentage of students' successes in the character education program will be considered satisfactory?

4. Will you be satisfied if efforts show that behaviors improve in school but have no effect on out-of-school behaviors?

5. Is there an expectation that once students have learned the core values, they will at least consider these values in the experiences that they will have in later life?

6. Is there an expectation that because of program efforts, the school will become more civil, compassionate, and challenging?

7. Has anyone asked the students what their expectations are for the character education program?

8. Is the character education program family based, school oriented, and community supported?

9. Is the program designed in such a way that the objectives have a good chance of being achieved over time?

10. Does the program have a comprehensive staff development and parent/family program?

The program standards and expectations are only two of the building blocks for the character education framework. A third building block is the set of criteria that should guide the work of the group and underscore the character education program in each school. We call these criteria the 11 C's for implementing effective council work and effective school programs. We will comment briefly on each criterion and assume that the leaders and other stakeholders will continually refer to these 11 criteria as they go about program planning, implementation, and assessment. We also assume that educators in schools with character education programs, or those who are contemplating instituting such programs, will attend to each of these criteria as well as to expectations for students. We believe that although all 11 criteria should be given equal attention, one stands out, and we list it first because of its importance.

Implementation Standards: The 11 C's

A *criterion* is a standard believed to have some certainty to it so that things may be judged by it. A *standard* is a measure of quantity, quality, or value established by general consent (Fernald, 1947, p. 142). The criteria described below have been selected to serve as standards that will guide the implementation of character education efforts. The criteria should also be viewed as standards that underscore programmatic efforts and environmental concerns in schools and communities (Figure 2.2).

Caring

Caring is the encompassing principle connecting such attributes as empathy, altruism, prosocial behavior, and efficacy (Chaskin & Rauner, 1995). Caring is a concept that has to permeate the organization from leaders to participants. The underpinning of the character education program is to show people of all ages that the community cares. Without a caring community, and adults who model the tenets of caring, all efforts to foster the consensus values and other benefits of character education programs simply will not work. We see the role of the council and other groups organizing the community to promote the theme of caring, to provide all community members opportunities to develop meaningful relationships, and to dem-

Figure 2.2. Implementation Criteria: The 11 C's

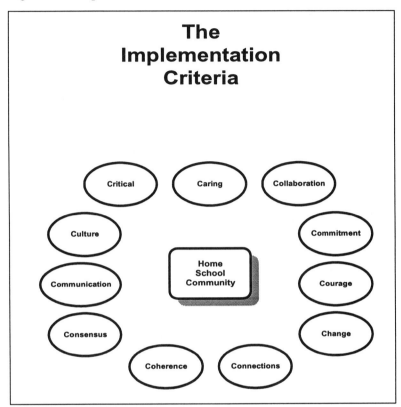

onstrate caring and sharing. Their job is to model prosocial behaviors, to highlight their intent that the community wants its children to be good learners, good human beings, and good citizens. For educators, that means from preschool to high school, children should learn and be encouraged to practice why caring, sharing, helping, and empathizing are good behaviors (Kohn, 1991).

Nel Noddings (1995) says that our society

needs to care for its children—to reduce violence, to respect hard work of every kind, to reward excellence at every level, to ensure a place for every child and emerging adult in the

economic and social world, to produce people who care com-
petently for their own families and contribute effectively to
their communities. (p. 366)

To restate the point—the principle of caring underpins both the
work of leaders and the work of stakeholders. It requires constant
attention by families, schools, the media, corporate and community
leaders, and community service providers. Consider the answer to
this question: If people don't care, why go through the exercise of
creating a character education program?

Collaboration

Chrislip and Larson (1994) provide direction on how citizens can
come together, under leadership that promotes and sustains collaboration, to solve problems. The authors define collaboration as "a
mutually beneficial relationship between two or more parties who
work toward common goals by sharing responsibility, authority, and
accountability for achieving results" (p. 5). Collaboration is based on
the premise that "if you bring the appropriate people together in
constructive ways with good information, they will create authentic
visions and strategies for addressing the shared concerns of the organization or community" (p. 14).

The Character Education Council that we envision is more than
cooperative. Council members are people who willingly work
together to create a common bond to accomplish missions and goals,
who practice participatory membership and shared leadership, who
support and work at creating a sense of community, and who willingly share responsibility for actions and hold each other accountable for the results of their efforts. Collaboration requires participants to engage in training and development activities, to clarify
roles, to take responsibility, to build trust, and to refuse to participate
in actions that detract from organizational unity, efficiency, and
effectiveness. Collaboration is absolutely essential for character education programs at the school site. Personnel must collaborate on
ways to infuse the values into the curriculum; on ways to celebrate
achievements; on ways to permeate the school's environment with a
caring, values-based experience for each child and adult in the

school; on ways to engage and involve families and the school's community; on ways to share leadership; and on ways to evaluate what works and what doesn't work.

Commitment

This criterion applies to individuals and groups who collaborate to create a community or school character education program. On the individual level, John Gardner (1990) says, "your identity is what you have committed yourself to—whether the commitment is to your religion, to an ethical order, to your work life, to loved ones, to the common good, or to coming generations" (p. 189). Individual commitment means preparing oneself for the sacrifices that will be demanded of one over time, which means having the physical and psychological energy to do so. It means learning as much about character education as one can so that contributions to the group's efforts will be maximized.

For a group, commitment means preparing for a common purpose, such as finding the ways and means to foster the consensus values (e.g., respect, responsibility, tolerance, self-discipline) in schools and in the community. It means accepting that there are no shortcuts to character education, that the group needs to be in for the "long haul." Long-term commitments by individuals and groups are essential to the success of a school's character education program. To do just this, school leaders must be committed to a vision of character education, and they must move others toward similar commitments (Gardner, 1990, p. 191).

Courage

All character education stakeholders will need to have courage. It takes courage to change, to take risks not knowing how things will turn out. It takes courage to face individuals and groups who challenge the purposes of character education. It takes courage to engage in discussion and debate. It takes courage to take a public stand on behalf of the tenets of the character education program. It takes courage to say enough is enough, to say we want our children and youth to learn and practice positive values and prosocial behaviors as counteragents to the negative behaviors they are learning from others in our society. And it takes courage to be held accountable for character education efforts.

For school leaders, it will take courage to share decision making; to empower others; to involve students in school governance; and to engage and involve parents and the community in the affairs of the school, particularly in the school's character education program. It will take courage to set high standards and hold all students accountable for reaching those standards. It will take courage to enforce, fairly, school rules and codes of conduct. It will take courage to be role models. It will take courage to change and to implement these 11 criteria.

Change

Character education means change—for the community, for families, and for schools. In character education, change is the school's and the community's attempts to educate children to become morally and socially literate. It is an attempt to reverse those conditions afflicting many of our children and youth that were described in Chapter 1. Change, although uncomfortable, opens up individuals and groups to new experiences, unexpected challenges, and new ways of knowing, feeling, and doing. Michael Fullan and Matthew Miles (1992) posed seven basic themes that should be contemplated by individuals and groups when thinking about and taking action. All seven involve change (look at character education as a synonym for "change" in this context):

1. "Change is learning" and is accompanied by "anxiety, difficulties, and uncertainty" (p. 749).

2. "Change is a journey, not a blueprint" that sends the message, "Do, then plan . . . and then plan some more" (p. 749).

3. Change is a "problem-rich process," and "problems are our friends" because problems "are the route to deeper change and deeper satisfaction" (pp. 749-750).

4. "Change is resource-hungry," demanding assistance and resources for training, time, space, and materials (p. 751).

5. "Change requires the power to manage it" and is best accomplished by a "cross-role group" (school personnel, students, and parents) at the school site that is empowered, cooperative, and collaborates with the school district office and community (p. 572).

6. "Change is systematic . . . [and] complex"; that is, it must focus on "structure, policy, and regulations" and also on the "deeper issues of the *culture* of the system" (pp. 751-752).

7. "Change is implemented locally"; that is, "*local* implementation by everyday teachers, principals, parents, and students is the only way change happens" (p. 752).

Connections

This criterion supports Chief Seattle's observation that "all things are connected." Life is a series of connections, and we feel that this criterion is particularly applicable to character education. We asked ourselves this question: Why do we encounter so much segregation, fragmentation, departmentalization, and separation? The public and the press seem to dwell on separation by race, ethnicity, gender, age, achievement, grades, subject matter, talents, abilities, politics, and income.

We suggest that for character education, we need to connect school and community groups. We need to connect the values of the program with the school's curriculum and activities program. We need to connect teachers with students; students with students; and teachers and students with parents and community members. We need to connect students with the literature of life, with heroes and heroines, and with appropriate role models. We need to connect schools with the community. We need to connect the character education program with other school intervention programs. We need to demonstrate to students how to connect the content of what they learn in one subject with the content learned in other subjects (integrated curriculum). We need to help students learn how to connect thinking with emotions and behaviors, how to connect learning with living, and how to connect in positive ways with parents, friends, and others in their lives. We are convinced that teachers and administrators need to connect with one another in new and better ways if character education programs are to be successful. We remind you that all these criteria are best applied to a character education framework when you and groups see them as connected.

Coherence

Edward Wynne (1988) studied 140 schools in the Chicago area and found that one of the major characteristics of "good" schools was coherence—"things sticking together." He reported that in these good schools, "the vitality of the total environment [coherence] stifled occasional surges of inefficiency" (p. 205). What we mean by coherence is attention by the leadership to promote and monitor the vitality, the togetherness, the interrelationships of all the components of the Character Education Council's interactions and work. For a school's character education program, coherence is the "glue" that relates what is happening in one grade or classroom to another, one program to another, and the unity of all the school's relationships and activities to each other. Coherence binds the consensus values to the daily life in the school. Coherence gives one the "big picture" of character education.

Consensus

The most important function of communities or school councils is to reach consensus on the democratic (personal and civic) values that they desire for their young. If the council can prioritize and clearly define these values, the council has greater likelihood of achieving their expectations, and the schools will have a much easier job implementing character education programs. Faith communities, schools, community organizations and businesses, the media, and families all play parts in shaping the character of the young, illustrating once again that the schools cannot do it alone. It does "take a village to raise a child." More than that, it takes a village working together. In a democracy, as many stakeholders as possible must involve themselves in the planning for a comprehensive character education program if the expectation is to raise children to have good character. The most successful programs are found where stakeholders take ownership of change efforts. Thus getting as many voices heard as possible is essential. This task is facilitated by using a consensus-building process for deciding on the personal and civic values that are priorities for character development in children and youth. We offer five tips to ensure reaching consensus:

1. Invite members of marginalized groups to join the community council and attend meetings.

2. Build trust among members. This may take time, but that time will be well spent. For example, you may bring in a consultant to conduct trust-building activities on site or during a retreat at a different location. Staff training activities that require cross-role collaboration also help bridge differences, enabling stakeholders to learn about each other's strengths as they complete interdependent tasks.

3. Get the commitment of group members to the goals of the community council. You can do this by having council members prepare and sign a goal statement, covenant, or manifesto.

4. Survey the membership of each organization in the council, as well as the general community, to be certain that many voices are heard and all opinions are considered.

5. Persist at the consensus effort and, even if only one value can be agreed upon, create and implement an action plan for that one value.

One or more districts within a community may work together to build consensus and an action plan for implementing a comprehensive program. The framework and the program standards we provided in this chapter are flexible, and they encourage each district and school to develop its own version of a character education program. In this way, all stakeholders have ownership in the process, thereby increasing the likelihood of the program reaching its goal.

Each stakeholder can put the rest of the 11 C's into practice after coming to consensus on the values to be fostered in the schools and community. Active involvement is facilitated by using consensus-building processes.

Communication

If these criteria are applicable to character education programs, then other people in and out of the daily operation of the program need to know what's going on and why. In planning and implementing character education programs in a language that the community understands, the mission and the expectations, and the styles and methods of delivery, are very important. The purpose of effective external communication is to build confidence, engender support, and encourage participation in the work of the council. Therefore some of the following conditions for effective communication require attention.

- *Policy:* Does the council have a written policy about its communication efforts that addresses both internal and public matters?

- *Roles:* Do group members know their roles? Do they know who is to do what and when they are to do it? Is it clear to each member what he or she can and should say as a council member and as a private party?

- *Specialists:* Does the council use the experts in their community— media people, marketing and promotion specialists, university researchers, companies whose work it is to poll the public—to help communicate with the public and particularly with parents? Because communication is a two-way process, these groups can help the council "hear" what the public is saying about their efforts and the programs being implemented.

- *Barriers:* Does the council attend to potential communication barriers? One obvious barrier can be the language of the people. Communication efforts must address the various languages that people speak in their homes and neighborhoods. Other barriers requiring attention include biases, prejudices, special interest groups, traditions, cultural heritages, and ways to deliver information.

୶ *Plans:* Does the council have well-developed communication plans? Are there plans for distribution of meeting minutes, for public bulletins, for intergroup communication, for newsletters, for a calendar of events, and for celebrations? Do the plans include ways for getting feedback from community groups, from parents and students, from critics and supporters, from leaders and participants?

Culture

Call it the school environment, culture, ethos or climate, or the hidden curricula—it must be based on the criteria of caring and consensus values that are central to the character education program. It would be enough to say that character education programs have no place in schools that have an environment where there is no clear vision or expectations, where there are nebulous objectives, job dissatisfaction, poor communication, student alienation and absenteeism, teacher apathy and low productivity, complaints and complacency, lack of creativity and innovation, little evidence of respect and trust, and a curriculum absent of enriching materials about values and ethics. Research and common sense tell us that if character education is to flourish in a school, those negative factors cannot exist. However, it may be that implementing a character education program will bring more positive influences to the daily life of a school.

It is not our intent here to provide a recipe for improving or enhancing school and classroom climates, nor is it our intent to develop detailed curriculum plans. Our intent is to call this criterion to your attention and to remind you that the community's consensus values should permeate the daily life of the school and its culture through its rites and rituals, codes and celebrations, curricula and cocurricular programs, classrooms and corridors, walls and windows, policies and procedures, symbols and stories, reports and recognitions, and operations and opportunities. It is the formal curriculum (cocurricular, special projects and programs), however, where the study and practice of the values, prosocial behaviors, and other character education content is formally learned and applied. The curriculum needs to be rich in the literature of values and ethics, in the history and traditions of a democracy. It needs to be centered in civics and focused on citizenship, with a strong emphasis on instructional practices that will stimulate and promulgate the habits of the mind (studying, moral reasoning, ethical decision making, creative and critical thinking, and evaluation) and of the heart (care, respect, concern, perseverance, responsibility, and acceptance). The character education curriculum, formal or hidden, should be connected with other efforts credited to help children and youth, such as substance abuse education, family life education, AIDS education, career education, life skills education, school-to-work programs, peer mediation, and community service learning.

Critical

The word *critical* comes from two Greek words: *kriticos*, meaning discerning judgment, and *kriterion*, meaning standards. The implication for the word *critical*, then, is to make judgments based on standards or on a set of criteria. The dictionary says that "critical, in its strictest sense, implies an attempt at objective judgment so as to determine both merits and faults."

We have stated throughout this book that educators need to be critical about what they say, what they do, and how they model the values that they are trying to foster. They need to make informed judgments about practices and promises. Educators need to discover and promote practices and strategies that work and discard those that do not work.

These criteria are not discrete; they are intertwined; they are connected! The listing of these 11 criteria is not exhaustive. Other criteria for organizational and programmatic effectiveness can be found in texts on the topic. Our intent is to alert you to some basic criteria that, if followed, can enhance the development and implementation of character education programs.

THE CHALLENGE

The telling is easy; the challenge is the doing. The challenge is in the implementing and sustaining of the school's character education program. The challenge is in keeping the people motivated and on task to accomplish the program's mission and goals. The challenge is accepting and creating change, applying the standards, and attending to the 11 C's in deciding next steps. The challenge is to apply the components of this comprehensive framework to the character education program you and others wish to create or maintain in your school and its community. Your challenge is to be courageous; to do those things that must be done, regardless of the barriers, to make your school a caring, civil, and challenging place for children and youth to learn and grow.

QUOTES:
Something to Think About

We can assume that renewed attention to character development will be good for pupils, their families, educators, and the nation. For, in the end, the welfare and the very existence of our society does not so much depend on the IQ's of its inhabitants, as on their character.

> —Wynne, E.(1986). Character development:
> Renewing an old commitment. Principal, 65(3), 31.

Schools provide children with a common meeting place in which to learn common values. As such, schools are the crucible where Americans are made and where children discover a heritage grown from a myriad of diverse cultures.

> —Block, A. (1996).
> Back to basics. California Journal, 27(6), 16.

There is an erroneous assumption, says Harold Howe II, a former U.S. Commissioner of Education, that "we can fix the schools so

*that schools can fix the kids, no matter how much we damage them
in families and communities that don't serve their needs."*

> —Steinberg, A. (Ed.). (1991). *What did you learn outside
> of school today?* The Harvard Education Letter, 7(4), 8.

QUESTIONS:
Something to Talk About

1. What school policies and procedures would you support to promote character education?

2. In your opinion, what kinds of action plans and activities might the schools in your community take to implement character education and to foster the community's consensus values?

3. How can school personnel create a school and classroom culture that will help foster the standards and criteria recommended in this chapter for a comprehensive character education program?

4. What role should students assume in your school's efforts to implement character education?

5. How might the 11 C's (criteria) in this chapter become part of the culture of your school? Your community?

BOOKS:
Something to Read About

Goodlad, J., Soder, R., & Sirotnik, K. (Eds.). (1990). *The moral dimensions of teaching.* San Francisco: Jossey-Bass.

Gutmann, A. (1987). *Democratic education.* Princeton, NJ: Princeton University Press.

Murphy, M. (1998). *Character education in America's blue ribbon schools.* Lancaster, PA: Technomic.

Starratt, R. J. (1996). *Transforming educational administration: Meaning, community, and excellence.* New York: McGraw-Hill.

PROGRAMS:
Something to Investigate

Character Plus, Formerly Personal Responsibility Education Process (PREP)

Program: PREP is a partnership of 22 districts, businesses, and community leaders working together to strengthen student responsibility, character, self-esteem, and academic achievement. PREP promotes a process that lets schools and communities rediscover their own values; that is, to determine which character traits it will focus on, which programs it will use, and how these programs will be implemented. PREP creates teams of trained teachers for each school site. Some of the programs are the "Student Portfolios Reinforced PREP"; "Math for S.U.R.E. (Students Using Responsible Education)"; "Service-Learning"; "PREP Student Task Force"; and "RAPP (Resolve All Problems Peacefully)."

Results: The findings of a study by Michael P. Grady provide evidence of effective implementation and institutionalization. However, student outcomes are mixed. Although PREP is rated highly by teachers, less than half reported seeing improvements in student behavior and in self-esteem. Only 25% of the participating students feel that students in their school respect one another. The researcher concluded that "there is no unambiguous and clear indication yet that PREP positively affects the behavior of the majority of students" (Moody & McKay, 1993, p. 6).

Contact: Linda McKay, Project Director, Cooperating School Districts, 8225 Florissant road, St. Louis, MO 63121; Tel: (314) 516-4522; Fax: (314) 516-4599.

Sweet Home School District, Amherst, New York

Program: This school district involved the entire community in developing a character education program that would reflect the needs of the community. The board of education incorporated character education into its mission statement. The character education program strives to promote a school climate that fosters among the students the development of civic and democratic values, such as respect and responsibility, and encourages students to make good decisions in their lives based on these values. A districtwide Values Education Council encourages each school in the district to develop its own character education programs using key districtwide character education factors.

Results: The comprehensive nature of the program, according to the district, makes it difficult to measure effectiveness. Yet the district does report that character education has been successfully integrated into the daily fiber of school life. Surveys of teachers, staff, parents, and students revealed an increase in the consciousness of the community about world problems, and students demonstrated their learnings in outreach and service activities within the school and the community. The program coordinator reported conversations with teachers, students, and administrators that indicate a keener awareness about the importance of being role models for others (Banas, S., 1996).

Contact: Director, Community Education Office, Sweet Home Central School District, 1901 Sweet Home Road, Amherst, NY 14228.

NOTES

1. Correspondence from Leslie Flanery, Coordinator of Intervention Services, Duncanville Independent School District, Duncanville, Texas.

2. Correspondence from Dot Woodfin, Coordinator, Character Education Program, Houston Independent School District, Houston, Texas.

3. Correspondence from Judith Casey, Principal, Antelope Trails Elementary School, Colorado Springs, Colorado.

CHAPTER 3

The Framework

Keys to Success

A school concerned with character development will help students develop senses of responsibility for what they think, say, and do. It will help develop their autonomy.

—Steven S. Tigner

Comprehensive character education programs are based on a vision of what ought to be, a set of expectations for stakeholders, program standards, and effective and efficient operating principles. Each of these elements is played out each day in each school in each community. Although not totally autonomous from the mission and mandates of the school district and from the culture of the community, each school, as an organization, will give its own unique "spin" to districtwide programs, policies, and procedures to meet the needs and interests of school site personnel, students, and their parents.

Because of this "autonomy," a community or school district's character education program must be interpreted and implemented by school site personnel. In fact, many districtwide character education programs encourage individual schools to approach implementation with creativity and imagination (see Character Plus, Chapter 2). Many schools have their own brand of character education programs because of the absence of districtwide initiatives. Some schools integrate character education programs into the existing curriculum. Others focus on a strategy labeled "value-a-month" or "value-a-week." Others foster values through a literature-based program. A few schools use a thematic approach. And then there are schools that have a comprehensive plan that implements a variety of strategies ranging from infusing character content into the curriculum, to student participation in school governance, to service learning opportunities. Programs and patterns vary; creativity and uniqueness reign.

Every new educational endeavor has external and internal factors that affect its implementation. To assist school site personnel, we have identified what we believe to be keys to successful character education programs. This chapter must be read, interpreted, and used within the context of the comprehensive character education framework described in the previous chapter. Because all three organizational patterns actually focus on what individual schools should be doing, we will focus on the "keys" that affect implementation at the school site level. The keys to success are leadership, expectations and consensus, school climate, implementation criteria, standards, training, partnerships, resources, and assessment.

We recognize that a school operates within a school district that may have a districtwide character education program in place. The character education director or coordinator for the district office is a major resource for assisting individual schools in implementing and sustaining character education programs. We expect that if there is a districtwide program, it will give some flexibility to the school sites. We assume that there will be districtwide events and activities in which an individual school should participate. Yet beyond the community and districtwide activities, it is the individual school site that holds the keys to successful character education initiatives.

KEY 1: LEADERSHIP

As we stated in the framework chapter, leadership is the first and one of the major components of a school's character education efforts. Leadership may emerge from members of the school council or from the community that the school serves. But the reality is that positional leadership is important to the program and thus the school principal plays a key leadership role. Some common tips for leaders of a school's character education program have emerged through workshops, seminars, academies, and conferences that we have participated in and from our conversations with teachers and administrators.

Ten Tips for Leaders

1. Leaders must create a mission statement and an organizational plan that implements the mission of the program.

2. Effective leaders empower others to lead and provide the resources and autonomy for others to "do the right thing," or what is ethical (Gardner, 1995).

3. Leaders create and support an environment of care and mutual trust, one that nurtures character education programs and practices.

4. Leaders use consensus-building strategies for making decisions about all elements of the school's character education program.

5. Leaders model the values of the program and coach others to be models as well.

6. Leaders create a school climate that nurtures the values of the program.

7. Leaders help others to cooperate, to collaborate, to trust one another, and to share responsibilities.

8. Leaders develop a communal sense of self-efficacy; that is, express sustained belief in the power of the community to achieve its goals (Starratt, 1996).

9. Leaders understand the importance of staff development and student-parent involvement.

10. Leaders thrive on feedback from evaluative efforts.

These 10 tips should help pave the way for your school to successfully implement and sustain its character education. The goal of the leaders in your school's character education program is to help students learn and practice the consensus values. The "heart of the American educational experience," says Jeremy Rifkin, president of the Foundation on Economic Trends, "is to give children a sense of possibility, a sense of opportunity, a sense that they can play a role in shaping their own destiny" (Mahaffey, 1999, p. 9). Our schools need leaders who can do just that!

Leadership must come from members of each of the school's character education committees and from the school administration, namely, the principal. We cannot say enough about the critical effect that leadership has on the effectiveness of a character education program. Schools and districts that are models of effectiveness have leaders that find time for staff to learn about character education and work through the instructional and programmatic elements by cooperating, collaborating, and creating. Effective leaders provide and maintain a vision for each school site that is based on values that are publicly agreed on. This vision must include and extend the consensus values. For example, if a school leader is applying Program Standard 2 (from Chapter 2), then that leader will be effective at communicating the vision to others within and outside the school. The larger work of effective school leaders is to engage all teachers, parents, and community members in the building of an ethical school. This includes providing an environment of support for character education programs and practices (Chapter 2 contains more detail about leadership).

KEY 2: EXPECTATIONS AND CONSENSUS

It is critical that you create clear goals, identify expectations, reach consensus, and apply standards to guide your efforts toward a comprehensive character education program. There are no national content standards currently under development for character education, so we encourage you to look at the program standards (see Chapter 2) we compiled as a guide, then create your specific goals and expectations related to character education. Each school site will have different priorities and, therefore, different goals and expectations.

A few expectations that cover a range of cognitive, affective, and behavioral factors, including the moral domain, follow.

Five Classroom Expectations

1. Build mutual trust and respect between teachers, students, and parents.

2. Model a classroom community of learners that supports the consensus values.

3. Provide direct instruction and discussion on the consensus values to help students learn about them, their definitions, and their importance.

4. Provide opportunities for students to practice the consensus values in realistic contexts.

5. Assess student learning objectives, provide feedback to students, and describe students' progress in formal reports to parents.

Student Learning Expectations

1. Demonstrate moral literacy (at developmentally appropriate levels) in the cognitive, affective, and behavioral domains (thinking, feeling, and doing).

2. Develop and demonstrate a sense of efficacy and self-respect.

3. Understand multiple perspectives and demonstrate empathetic concern for the welfare of others.

4. Apply skills in moral reasoning and ethical decision making to solve problems.

5. Demonstrate mastery of the skills of social cooperation (fairness, respect for others, kindness, courtesy, responsibility, etc.).

6. Take responsibility for their own learning, become independent learners, and exhibit a positive attitude toward school and class work.

These expectations were adapted from the Child Development Project (see Chapter 5). Your school site committee may want to review these expectations, adapt or modify them, and create others to fit their own circumstances.

Reaching Consensus

One of the basic premises of the framework, you will recall, is the necessity for a community or school council to reach consensus on the personal and civic values desired for the students at the school. If the council can prioritize and clearly define these values, it has a greater likelihood of achieving its expectations, and the school will have a much easier job implementing a character education program. To avoid problems during implementation, we suggest that the council follow Gutmann's recommendations about practicing democratic principles, and when coming to consensus, weigh their choices on the principles of nondiscrimination and nonrepression. Community involvement is essential because, according to Gutmann (1987), "the policies that result from democratic deliberations [in a community council] will be more enlightened by the values and concerns of the representatives of the many communities that constitute a democracy" (p. 11).

Democratic principles alone will not be sufficient to ensure that the council's day-to-day operations are efficient and effective. In

Chapter 2, we offer some guiding criteria ("11 C's") that, if practiced, may guarantee success and ensure that a school or a district will be a model for character education. Each stakeholder can put the 11 C's into practice as they create the mission and action plan for their school and community.

KEY 3: SCHOOL CLIMATE

The hidden curriculum consists of the events, situations, and incidents that occur on a regular basis that may be planned or unplanned, anticipated or unanticipated. The overall school climate is a reflection of all the combined aspects of the hidden curriculum and its effects on all the people who enter the school. School climate is a major factor affecting character education because it can negate the effects of any formal program. The research on school climate over the past 20 or so years leads us to make the following recommendations:

- ∽ The school climate includes rules and procedures, rewards and penalties, assemblies and honors, and positive working relationships between staff, faculty, parents, and administration. This climate, to foster the consensus values in students, must encompass the 11 C's outlined in Chapter 2.

- ∽ The hidden curriculum is as important as the formal curriculum to students learning values. People's "actions speak louder than their words" (Williams, 1993). To learn the consensus values, children and youth need to see significant adults modeling these values daily.

- ∽ The physical plant should be safe and clean. It doesn't have to be shiny and new, just a pleasant and safe place to work. Research suggests that working conditions that are attractive, pleasant, and safe contribute to the achievement, performance, and motivation of the staff and students (Starratt, 1996).

৵ High expectations of success permeate an effective school's climate. According to Starratt (1996), high expectations extend to effort and cooperation as well as to performance. Successes are celebrated regularly in award ceremonies and special assemblies.

৵ The faculty, staff, and administration take responsibility for the outcomes of the school's character education efforts. Stakeholders treat poor or negative results of the character education program as problems to be solved and opportunities for improvement.

According to Starratt (1996), stakeholders in an effective school identify goals, marshal their resources, establish a process by which goals can be achieved, create a strong consensus that they can do something, and commit themselves to doing it. The overall school climate radiates a culture that communicates the organization's values to others within and outside the school community (see Chapter 4).

KEY 4: IMPLEMENTATION CRITERIA

The implementation criteria described in Chapter 2 serve as standards that guide the implementation of character education efforts. These criteria are caring, collaboration, commitment, courage, change, connections, coherence, consensus, communication, culture, and critical. These criteria underscore programmatic and assessment efforts and environmental concerns in schools and communities. These criteria, if followed, can enhance the development, implementation, and assessment of comprehensive character education programs and practices.

KEY 5: STANDARDS

Standards allow stakeholders to focus on essential elements of development, implementation, and assessment. Standards provide guidelines and benchmarks for educators interested in ensuring quality programs and results. Standards are so important that we have developed six sets of standards that are described and discussed throughout this book: program standards and implementation standards (Chapter 2), teaching standards (Chapter 4), partnership standards (Chapter 5), assessment standards (Chapter 6), and the curriculum standards that follow.

Curriculum Standards

It is not our intention to endorse a particular program or set of curriculum materials. Whether you develop your own materials or use prepackaged materials, there are a number of guidelines that can help you choose the program that will fit with your consensus values, school goals, and program expectations. When starting out, it is difficult to determine which curriculum is the right one for your district or school. It is confusing because there are so many different programs making similar claims. You should not have to call in curriculum specialists to make the decisions for your school site committee. You can use the curriculum standards we provide here as guidelines to evaluate character education curricula. We have included a simple rating scale to guide your evaluation.

Curriculum Standard 1. The character education curriculum fosters the consensus values of the community and matches the goals and expectations of the character education program.

Curriculum Standard 2. The curriculum can be incorporated into or integrated with existing state or district content syllabi or subject matter frameworks. If you use a curriculum that someone else has developed or published, time will be needed for school personnel to adapt the curriculum materials.

Curriculum Standard 3. The character education curriculum can easily be adapted and revised to use with different students in different school sites. The expectations of the program are clear enough and the goals are broad enough to be applied to a variety of settings, even within the same community.

Curriculum Standard 4. The character education curriculum materials include a separate guide for teachers, providing sample daily or unit plans, questions to ask students, potential classroom activities to integrate into content lessons, strategies for parents, and assessment criteria.

Curriculum Standard 5. The character education curriculum promotes critical thinking in students. Students should be required to use ethical decision-making and moral-reasoning skills when evaluating problems or issues. The problems or issues should be developmentally appropriate and intrinsically motivating, providing rich and varied contexts for students to apply these skills across content areas.

Curriculum Standard 6. The character education curriculum should require students to put into practice the consensus values. Curriculum materials that include hands-on activities that encourage students to practice what they have learned about the consensus values are greatly desired over materials that do not. Some examples of this are materials that engage students in cooperative group processing with peers and cocurricular activities that extend to service learning within or outside the school community.

Curriculum Standard 7. The character education curriculum does not contain any materials or references that are biased toward any group. An examination should be made of the perspectives of the authors, the packaging of materials, and the language and style of the written and graphic materials, in addition to the content of the curriculum.

The following rating scale can be used to guide your evaluation of curriculum materials:

Rating Scale for Character Education Curriculum

0–2: Meets or attempts to meet up to two of the curriculum standards (not recommended)

3–4: Meets or attempts to meet three to four of the curriculum standards (consider—major adaptations)

5–6: Meets or attempts to meet five to six of the curriculum standards (satisfactory—some adaptations)

7: Meets or exceeds all the curriculum standards (excellent match)

We recommend that you use these curriculum standards as a guide when you evaluate character education curriculum or create your own. Finding a satisfactory or an excellent match between your goals and expectations and the curriculum used may take time, but it is time well spent. In the end, the most powerful, meaningful, and effective curriculum may not be a packaged program; instead it may be an infused program, one created by staff at the school site where it will be used.

Curriculum Infusion

Taking curriculum guides and materials developed by teachers at one school and adapting them to your local setting may not be as effective as developing your own materials and plans on site. Why? Because your consensus values and curriculum frameworks, and your goals and expectations for a character education program, may be different from those in the prepared program. We believe that any prepared curriculum materials may have less of an impact than "homemade" curriculum. This is true for curriculum in most areas but is especially true when dealing with character education. It is important that teachers implement curriculum for which they take ownership. Creating the character education curriculum on site may be the best way to bring teachers and other school personnel in as stakeholders. It is also an effective training strategy. Character education should be integrated as much as possible into existing curriculum frameworks, and that is difficult to do with packaged materials. Nevertheless, prepared curriculum materials can be effective if they meet all or most of the curriculum standards described in this chapter.

To be most effective, character education activities must be infused throughout school and classroom practices and processes (i.e., the formal and the hidden curriculum). Treated separately, out of context, character education curriculum materials and programs are likely to have minimal effect on students. For example, studies by Good and Brophy (1991) on moral reasoning indicate that students exposed to ethical dilemmas, and who are trained to use moral reasoning skills to interpret those dilemmas, have shown increased abilities in moral reasoning. Yet there is no evidence that these skills are transferred beyond the intellectual realm into students' personal beliefs or actions (pp. 160-192). If character education curricular materials are comprehensively infused into a school that has a caring and cooperative school climate (note the 11 C's), provides a safe and risk-free environment for students and teachers, and has school leaders that carry the vision forward and encourage the kinds of activities we recommend in the program standards in Chapter 2, the program should be successful. An effective comprehensive character education program then is infused throughout all aspects of life in the school. It is not treated as an isolated curricular or program intervention.

Cocurriculum

Character is developed in schools through its climate, curriculum, cocurricular activities, services, and the daily interactions between people. Each of these elements should help students come to "know the good" (educate their minds). But that, in itself, is not enough. Knowing the good, using one's mind well, is just one side of the character coin. The other side adds to the value of the coin— helping students become good persons by helping them practice what they know about the good, about right and wrong. The result is to educate their minds and hearts.

What happens through the curriculum in individual classrooms is only one aspect of a student's experience in schools. The cocurriculum refers to the activities that are in addition to the regular or formal curriculum of the school. Sometimes cocurricular activities become part of the formal curriculum; community service learning is an example. A whole realm of cocurricular activities exists at school that can have a tremendous influence on the learning of values by children and youth. Cocurricular activities can contribute to helping students develop self-discipline and self-esteem, cooperation and teamwork, respect and responsibility, and a sense of belonging and contribution. In many cases, the cocurricular program is a place where students can practice and apply the consensus values and develop good character traits. From sports to school clubs and publications, the opportunities are plentiful. It is important to get as many adults as possible involved with youth in cocurricular activities. The questions to ask are, Do the adults responsible for coaching, advising, and monitoring these programs see themselves as part of the school's character education efforts? Have they been given the responsibility by the school's character education committee to determine how the activity for which they are responsible contributes to the expectations of the character education program? What follows are some examples of cocurricular programs and activities that can be used to enhance character education throughout the school.

Student Council. Although the degree of involvement will vary according to the age and grade level of the students, council members should be aware of their active involvement in the school's character education efforts. Students should be represented on school committees when appropriate.

Publications. School publications, such as newspapers, yearbooks, magazines, classroom newspapers, and other student publications will provide opportunities for students to apply the consensus values, including teamwork, cooperation, responsibility, tolerance, and the like. Students working in this arena, particularly those working on the school newspaper, face the ethical issues of rights and responsibilities, censorship and freedom of the press, taste and tact. Students and their advisers might ask how the school's publications could help promote the character education efforts.

Athletics. For physical education, the experts agree that the following should be included as a primary objective: The student has social skills and a positive self-concept (Pangrazi & Dauer, 1995). There are two kinds of athletic programs that allow students to show their physical talents, to learn new skills, and to practice the values of the character education program—intramural and interscholastic sports. What better venue to teach the values of teamwork, cooperation, persistence, patience, self-discipline, and perseverance? What better place is there for students to witness these values exhibited by adults in charge, the coaches and mentors? The school's character education committee should give special attention to have the school's athletic programs help foster the consensus values. There is a gold mine of opportunities here that should not go untapped.

Service Learning. "Learning to serve our communities—for the good of all—is one of the most rewarding school lessons" (Parsons, 1996, p. 11). Service learning is the best way we can think of for schools to operationalize character education. Students need an opportunity to practice what they are learning about the consensus values. In short, students learn values by practicing them. Service learning experiences can have the most powerful long-term effect on students' behavior and attitudes. To gain the most out of service learning, we recommend that it be guided, that the placements be developmentally appropriate, and that the experiences be meaningful ones for the students. Reflection is absolutely essential for processing the experience and must be included as part of the requirements.

School Services. There are an array of services that one finds in schools and school districts. For example, there are health services, guidance and psychological services, social work, speech and hearing services, services for exceptional students, custodial and secretarial services, and food and transportation services. The responsibilities of those working as school service providers are

- Awareness of the school's character education efforts

- Membership on the various character education committees

- Identification of their role, responsibilities, and potential contributions to the program

- Working with educators and others to promote the consensus values

- Participation in special events, celebrations, and recognitions

- ✍ Promotion of the value of their service to the school's academic and character education program
- ✍ Assisting the school administration in informing the parents and the community about the program
- ✍ Creating a team effort in all phases of the character education program and the school service programs

KEY 6: TRAINING

Training, as we refer to it in the framework, refers to effective instructional strategies that can be learned through inservice staff development programs and activities. Instruction and staff development both apply to the classroom level (see Chapter 4 for more on training).

Instruction

Teaching is essentially a moral craft (Tom, 1984), and all interactions between students and teachers contain moral elements. Teachers need to be aware of this fact and accept their role as character educators. The instructional strategies that make a difference in students' learning of the consensus values are the ones that facilitate and guide students from analysis to applications, giving them opportunities to put their knowledge of the values into practice and encouraging them to become both independent and collaborative learners. The most effective teaching strategies are constructive; that is, they enable students to construct their own understanding of the consensus values. Over the past 20 years, we have learned from research in educational psychology that the transmission model (teachers as lecturers) is not the best way to enhance student learning. Instead, teachers must motivate and empower diverse students in ways that enable them to be meaningfully engaged. Teachers must make content meaningful and relevant to students' lives, giving students opportunities to explore, create, and apply in ways that intrinsically motivate them to want to know more about the subjects they are studying. Students will learn the value of learning, build self-esteem, and become independent learners as they learn the values of responsibility, persistence, self-respect, respect for others, and the like.

Over the years, observing in schools and classrooms, we have noted some outstanding classroom practices that teach both character and content to students (i.e., educating their hearts and minds). According to Wynne and Ryan (1997), the most effective schools do both; they enable students to attain high levels of cognitive learning and good character. When students are fair, honest, responsible, and respectful, for example, they also score higher on standardized and other achievement tests (Schaps, Watson, & Lewis, 1996). There are essential instructional principles that all educators can use to create an effective classroom climate and to ensure that students go beyond content and learn the consensus values.

Staff Development

As we emphasized earlier, before program plans are implemented, there need to be efforts to provide staff (those who are expected to implement and sustain the program) with opportunities to learn more about character education—its literature and research; effective instructional methods; issues and concerns surrounding school attempts at character education; the importance of modeling desired behaviors; and applying the keys that lead to successful character education initiatives. Training models that include staff development strategies on effective instructional methods are presented more fully in Chapter 4.

KEY 7: PARTNERSHIPS

Networking with others who are implementing character education is a great help. However, more widespread success can be found in the partnerships with parents, faith community leaders, social service agency representatives, and businesses that are developed through the character education initiatives. Partnerships with individuals and organizations interested in character education are invaluable; they are so important that we have devoted Chapter 5 to it.

KEY 8: RESOURCES

Comprehensive character education programs should benefit from the rich variety of resources that are available in each community. It is important that resources (texts, programs, lesson plans, and assessment instruments) be made available to those who are planning and implementing the character education program. There are a number of programs and materials that have been created and are available for review (see "Programs: Something to Investigate," at the end of each chapter). The most comprehensive clearinghouse of materials, programs, and assessment instruments is the Web site hosted by the Character Education Partnership: http://www.character.org.

KEY 9: ASSESSMENT

If you decide to create your own goals, objectives, and action plans, remember to make them clear enough and specific enough so that you can assess them. We recommend strongly that you consider how you are going to assess the impact of a character education program or practices in as comprehensive a way as possible. For you to be able to report successes back to the community, you need to be systematic and thorough in gathering data to confirm the degree and quality of your successes at reaching goals and objectives (see Chapter 6).

QUOTES:
Something to Think About

The primary responsibility for our schools should be to nurture and enhance the wit (mind and intellect) and the character of the young. Both wit and character are vital to this nation and to the individuals who comprise it.

— Graham, P. A. (1984). Schools: Cacophony about practice, silence about purpose. Daedalus, 113(4), 49.

An excellent school struggles with the ethical ambiguities and tensions in contemporary life and engages its members with the burden of the effort to live morally in a community.

— *Starratt, R. (1996).* Transforming educational administration: Meaning, community, and excellence. *New York: McGraw-Hill, p. 173.*

States, parents, and professional educators all have important roles to play in cultivating moral character. A democratic state of education recognizes that educational authority must be shared among parents, citizens, and professional educators.

— *Gutmann, A. (1987).* Democratic education. *Princeton, NJ: Princeton University Press, p. 42.*

QUESTIONS:
Something to Talk About

1. Can schools become model democratic institutions, given their organizational structure, political position, and historical record?

2. What keys to success would you add to the list of the nine described in this chapter?

3. What recommendations would you have for character education leaders in your school and community for creating successful programs?

4. What is your feeling about prepackaged programs and the "do-it-yourself" idea?

5. Are there additional curriculum standards that you would add to the seven we presented in this chapter?

BOOKS:
Something to Read About

Benninga, J. (Ed.). (1991). *Moral character and civic education in the elementary school.* New York: Teachers College Press.

Nucci, L. (Ed.). (1989). *Moral development and character education: A dialogue.* Berkeley, CA: McCutchan.

Tom, A. R. (1984). *Teaching as a moral craft.* New York: Longman.

Williams, M., & Schaps, E. (Eds.). (1999). *Character education: The foundation for teacher education* (Report of the ATE National Commission on Character Education). Washington, DC: Character Education Partnership.

PROGRAMS:
Something to Investigate

The Heartwood Program

Program: This literature-based ethics curriculum is designed to foster, in children from kindergarten through the sixth grade, seven universal values: courage, loyalty, justice, respect, hope, honesty, and love. Coupled with a teacher-training component and a teacher's manual, the program proposes addressing one attribute per month through the use of a kit containing 14 books (2 for each attribute), activity cards, a world map of the countries represented in the classic multicultural children's stories from around the world, and a resource manual for teachers.

Results: A 1990-1991 report of implementation in seven elementary schools by Marina Piscolish (Research and Evaluation Coordinator on the Pittsburgh Public Schools) showed that teachers were overwhelmingly positive about the program and its materials, and for the freedom and flexibility it provides. Students and teachers stated that the program seemed to influence classroom climate and relationships. Student responses indicated personal knowledge and understanding of the attributes and their application. Another study conducted by Research for Better Schools in 1991-1992 for the Pennsylvania Department of Education, Division of Federal Programs field-tested the program in 16 districts in Pennsylvania. Major findings suggest that teachers believed there is a need for such a program: it is "teacher-friendly"; it provided "a constructive strategy for initiating discussions with students"; it worked best when used on a consistent and interdisciplinary basis; teacher training should be more intensive to assist teachers in using the materials; and the program enhanced students' in-depth discussions and understanding of the seven attributes. A third study (Leming, 1998) found consistent and strong curriculum effects with regard to cognitive understanding. After only one year, Heartwood students at all grade levels were better able to define and recognize instances of the attributes. Results on the other two variables were more mixed, for example, the curriculum significantly improved respect for diversity among Caucasian students in grades 1-3, but not among older students. Teachers reported improved conduct at all grade levels, but the data suggest interaction effects with teacher and classroom variables such as moral character of the teacher and attitudes toward the curriculum.

Contact: Eleanore N. Childs, President, The Heartwood Ethics Institute, 425 N. Craig Street, Suite 302, Pittsburgh, PA 15213, Tel: (412) 688-8570.

School-Site Values Curriculum: PS31

One example curriculum was developed by teams of elementary school teachers at PS31—William Lloyd Garrison School, in the South Bronx, New York City. One of the authors, Mary Williams, was called upon as a resource, guide, and facilitator for program development. What follows is a list of steps taken at the school to plan and prepare for their character education program.

Step 1:

The school and community agreed on the values that they would foster in the school. The list was generated, values were defined, and because there were a large number of consensus values, a value-of-the-week program was started to "do something" at the start of the new school year.

Step 2:

A university character education specialist was brought in on an inservice training day to share the local and national imperative for character education and to help the teachers create a framework of teaching characteristics they could use to guide their program development and implementation; the specialist also helped to bridge the gap between teaching content and teaching character.

Step 3:

The teachers and school specialists, along with the principal, began to review the existing content syllabi mandates, curriculum materials, texts, and previous unit plans devised by teams of teachers. Their objective was to see where the consensus values already fit in and find other places where they could be integrated.

Step 4:

As a result of Step 3, teams of teachers decided that new unit plans needed to be created in order to integrate the consensus values into the state- and city-mandated content curricula.

Step 5:

Meetings were held to prepare teams of teachers for planning; the teams really got started as study groups. References were gathered, distributed, read, and discussed in the following areas: thematic units, curriculum integration, high-level-thinking questions, and character education.

Step 6:

Grade-level teams of teachers (grades 1–2, 3–4, 5–6) went to work to integrate character into the content of their curriculum:

- The social studies topics became the unit themes for each grade level.

- The English/language arts curriculum was matched with the appropriate social studies themes.

- Writing across the curriculum was integrated into lessons.

- As consensus values emerged from the literature and social studies themes, they were highlighted.

- Questions were created for teachers to ask students that would encourage them to consider and reflect on the values embedded in the content.

- All units and sample lesson plans followed the STAR lesson-plan approach that the teachers had been using for a few years. (They include special appendixes in the guide for the STAR lesson plan, graphic organizers, literature bibliographies, and references for thematic units.)

- Higher order thinking questions were created and included with the lesson plan for each grade level to serve as representative samples in the curriculum guide.

This homemade curriculum matched the school's consensus values to mandated content syllabi and, at the same time, it brought teachers in as stakeholders in the character education program. Character education was not an add-on—it was integrated as much as possible into the existing curriculum.

Contact: Carol Russo, Principal, PS31–William Lloyd Garrison School, 425 Grand Concourse, Bronx, NY 10451; Tel: (718) 292-4397.

CHAPTER 4

cɔⓞⓞɔ

Training

Instruction and Staff Development

The unexamined life is not worth living.

—Socrates

Instruction is to character education what the heart and mind are to the body. No matter how comprehensive a character education program may look on paper, if the teachers do not have the interest, knowledge, and skills to implement the program, then it is just another program taking up shelf space.

Training, used in the comprehensive framework, refers to everything related to classroom teaching. Training includes all instructional elements and staff development in schools. We offer several recommendations in this chapter that will ensure quality training to enhance the instructional strategies used by teachers, which will ultimately result in both higher academic achievement and character development in students.

We begin with some suggestions from an administrator and a researcher. Next, we propose a set of teaching standards that can serve as a benchmark for teachers in your character education program. These standards also provide hints about teacher preparation, roles, and responsibilities. Then we talk about teaching principles that have an effect on classroom climate, with an emphasis on modeling. We also offer the "5 C's"—teaching strategies—that we and others suggest are important to the teaching of values. The chapter ends with some comments about the importance of training and tips regarding the types of training and staff development strategies we have found to be successful.

Instruction consists of a variety of elements. All the recommendations we make related to training are based on the research on children's moral development. According to Eric Berger (1996), the K–12 character education program of Locust Valley Central School District, New York, is based on nine ethical values (honesty/integrity, respect, courtesy, self-discipline, compassion, tolerance, love of learning, respect for education, and responsibility) and is consistent with 10 clues from the research on children's moral development.

Children develop a commitment to ethical values from

1. Identifying with significant others who live by these values

2. Internalizing these values from others

3. Learning to love the good in oneself

4. Experiencing reinforcement of behaviors demonstrating these values

5. Experiencing logical consequences from adults for behaviors opposing these values

6. Seeing models who exemplify these values

7. Developing perspective taking

8. Acquiring higher levels of moral reasoning

9. Experiencing these values in relationships and interactions

10. Practicing behaviors exemplifying these values (p. 3)

Clues from the research also help focus this chapter on the "best" practices, or what has been found to be successful. In the previous three chapters, we outlined a framework that included the building blocks for a comprehensive character education program: leadership, expectations and consensus, climate, implementation criteria, standards, training, partnerships, resources, and assessment. It is now time to look at instruction as reported by those who day-to-day administer, instruct, and evaluate efforts to improve students' prosocial behaviors; assist at-risk students; enhance students' academic skills and abilities; and foster character development. This chapter, then, is about facts as we know them at this time. It is about findings, as limited as they may be. It is about findings that character education and other behavioral intervention efforts may counter some students' negative behaviors, assist at-risk children and youth, and address the appalling statistics reported in Chapter 1.

EXPERT TESTIMONY

According to Leming (1993b), what we have learned so far about effective character education is this:

- Didactic methods alone—codes, pledges, teacher exhortation, and the like—are unlikely to have any significant or lasting effect on character.

- The development of students' capacity to reason about questions of moral conduct does not result in a related change in conduct. Apparently, one cannot reason one's way to virtuous conduct.

- Character develops within a social web or climate. The nature of that environment, the messages it sends to individuals, and the behaviors it encourages and discourages are important factors to consider in character education. Clear rules of conduct, student ownership of those rules, a supportive environment, and satisfaction resulting from complying with the norms of the environment shape behavior.

- Character educators should not expect character formation to be easy (p. 69).

Leming (1993a) has also published a booklet, essential reading for all character educators, in which he reviews past and current research on moral-values education programs, on the potential of the schools to foster students' character development, and on the merits of schools' intervention-education programs, from which he offers several conclusions:

- ✍ Character-related behaviors will not change as a result of moral dilemma strategies or moral discussion strategies.

- ✍ Some prosocial character traits will result from cooperative learning environments.

- ✍ Limited, but important, positive changes in student character results from school and classroom climates that embody clear standards, mutual respect between teachers and students, and shared governance.

- ✍ Encouraging results have been found when there is clear communication among stakeholders and support by peers and the community for appropriate behaviors (p. 16).

- ✍ Factors that are most significant in school efforts to foster character include the school atmosphere (not the formal school curricula and traditional approaches), personal characteristics of teachers, the teacher's role, teacher-student relationships, and the classroom climate (p. 20).

- ✍ Clear and fairly enforced rules, an orderly school environment and classroom climate, and interventions (with definition and support of appropriate behaviors) that incorporate students, parents, and the community contribute to the development of character and prosocial behaviors (p. 23).

We will devote the next part of this chapter to instructional strategies that have been found to be effective. The findings and feelings reported here underscore the importance of the framework outlined in the two previous chapters. Training in effective instructional strategies is just one of the elements of a successful school program. Studies show that the teacher's role has the most significant effect on a program's success (Leming, 1998; Lewis, Schaps, & Watson, 1995). Effective instructional strategies are the foundation for the staff development tips we describe later in the chapter.

INSTRUCTION

New models of teaching effectiveness (ones that encourage teachers to create mutually respectful, student-centered learning communities that engage students in meaningful, relevant learning tasks) also build good character. The National Commission on the Moral and Ethical Dimensions of Teaching (1996) endorse having teachers teach and model the values of morality, responsibility, and excellence in their classrooms and schools. Yet there have been few studies that have examined classroom instruction at the level required for analyzing how students learn moral values. One study (Williams, 1993) examined how students construct understanding about respect for others within the context of their classroom. The study found that the teachers who are most effective at teaching values to students are the ones who create a learning community (a positive classroom climate) that engages students in relevant learning tasks, in which students are able to work at developmentally appropriate levels, both alone and collaboratively with others. In addition, the most effective teachers are the ones who model the values they want their students to learn. Some guiding principles for effective character education that emerged from that study follow.

Six Instructional Principles for
Effective Character Educators

1. Create a community of learners in your classroom.
2. Be hardworking and really care about student learning.
3. Create a climate of mutual trust and respect (an ethic of care).
4. Create a collaborative and supportive learning environment.
5. Act consistently according to stated intentions.
6. Model the behavior students are expected to follow.

MODELING

Of these six instructional principles, modeling deserves a few comments. Modeling is an essential component of a comprehensive character education program and is found in both the school climate and classroom environment. In the past, sharing one's personal values and modeling have been considered too personal to be included in the classroom; thus many educators have believed that it is better to be neutral and not get involved in teaching values in school. For decades, educators have felt comfortable with programs like values clarification where they could avoid issues like modeling and instead focus on teaching the content and the mechanics of instruction (see Chapter 1). Taking this kind of relativistic stand has a negative effect on students because the effects of modeling are so powerful that students who learn the wrong message—that values are unimportant or that all personal beliefs and values are acceptable—may end up getting hurt. Each adult is a model for children and has an impact on them—for good or bad.

Teacher modeling is perhaps the most powerful of all the factors that affect character education. The National Association of Secondary School Principals' 1996 document, *Breaking Ranks,* lists as their second recommendation: "Teachers should model the ethics and values considered essential in a democratic and civil society." Educators teach values to students, whether they want to or not. Students learn from the types of assignments teachers give and from the types of interactions they have with other adults in the school. If there is a mismatch between what adults do and what they say, students will imitate what is done. Students may actually ignore or reject what teachers say if it does not fit with students' observations of what they do (Williams, 1992). Educators cannot turn off their modeling effects at will. They need to be aware of the effect of their behavior on students. The statements, "Actions speak louder than words," and "Walking the talk," should not be taken lightly. Modeling is a powerful learning medium because it will either reinforce or negate what is learned through the formal curriculum and cocurricular activities.

CLASSROOM CLIMATE

Attention to creating a positive classroom climate takes priority over any other practice or process in character education. The classroom climate, like the school climate, has a significant effect on student behavior because students learn more from what their teachers do than what their teachers say. A positive classroom climate reflecting an environment that supports a community of learners is a desirable outcome and precursor of effective character education.

Here are a few key questions that the school's character education committee and stakeholders need to discuss about the classroom climate:

- ✍ Is there anything in this classroom environment that detracts from the values and goals of the character education initiatives being planned?

- ✍ Is there anything in the way this teacher is organized that will promote or detract from the expectations and outcomes of the character education programs?

- ✍ Should lesson plans, rules, and procedures be examined to determine the extent to which they support or detract from program expectations?

- ✍ Are current teacher-to-student interactions and student-to-student interactions such that they foster the consensus values and support program expectations?

The classroom climate has an enormous influence on students—in both their academic achievement and in character education. Positive or negative values are taught throughout the school day, during and between formal lessons. Teachers need to attend to creating a sense of community in the classroom, where mutually respectful relationships are nurtured and prosocial behaviors welcomed and rewarded.

STANDARDS

After program implementation begins, the leadership must help participants find time to come together to discuss progress; to reflect on the consensus values and their infusion into the schools' climate and formal curriculum; to examine new information; to ask questions and seek answers to what is working, what is not, and why. In other words, school-site plans must include ongoing staff development efforts. To guide educators in all aspects of instruction and staff development, we offer the following teaching standards for character education.

Teaching Standards for Character Education

Standard 1. New and experienced teachers need to practice and reflect on their role as character educators responsible for the character formation of all students.

Standard 2. Teachers need to understand their roles and responsibilities as value transmitters, value critics, and role models and communicate high expectations for all students regarding prosocial behaviors, character development, and democratic values. They should strive, along with students, to eliminate behaviors that are antithetical to good character.

Standard 3. Teachers must help create school and classroom climates that emulate mutual respect and support the tenets of a community of learners (e.g., being caring, being cooperative, being civil).

Standard 4. Teachers need to engage all students in ethical analysis, critical inquiry, and higher order thinking skills as they pursue ethical dilemmas found in literature, history, media, and life.

Standard 5. Teachers need to work with colleagues, students, parents, and community groups to develop character lessons that will provide positive value experiences as a part of the schools' curricular and cocurricular programs.

Standard 6. Understand that parents are their children's primary character educators. Knowing that the community, peer groups, and the media have a major influence on the character development of the young, teachers need to form collaborative partnerships between home, school, and the community that welcome and involve others in character development efforts. (Adapted from "Character Education: A One-Act Play" by E. F. DeRoche, 1999, *Action in Teacher Education, 20*(4), 100–107.)

Educators who attend to these standards will find the tasks of integrating the character education aspects of schooling much easier. Teaching standards can help both new and veteran teachers and can be useful as tools for school administrators to measure teacher effectiveness in this area.

CLASSROOM STRATEGIES

Next, we will share tried-and-true classroom strategies that enable students to reach high levels of academic achievement and build character. The Five C's are interrelated and, when used in combination, present a powerful combination of strategies that foster character education. Nevertheless, we will examine each one separately.

The Five C's

☐ **Classroom management**

☐ **Conflict resolution**

☐ **Cooperative learning**

☐ **Citizenship**

☐ **Critical thinking**

Classroom Management

What is classroom management? Classroom management is linked directly to classroom climate, as described earlier in this chapter. The rules and procedures, rewards and punishments, seating charts, and other classroom arrangements are all included in classroom management. Classroom management is one of the biggest concerns of teachers, and we list it first because it is inclusive and affects the other strategies. One method we have found to be effective in creating a positive management system is to include student input through class meetings. This also promotes a positive, nurturing, supportive classroom climate. Class meetings will link directly to citizenship lessons because students have opportunities to practice putting democratic principles into action. Classroom discipline policies may include peer mediation and conflict-resolution strategies to make them stronger. But before we jump ahead, a word about class meetings.

Class meetings are a powerful example of classroom management strategies that can foster the goals of a character education program. When reflecting on class meetings, a couple of critical ideas emerge. What you see in class meetings is a ritual that helps students think beyond themselves. What is hoped for is discussion, insight, and commitment. It is a ritual that attempts to build a sense of community and it doesn't always have to be a class meeting—it can be an advisory group, a student council, a peer-group meeting, or a face-to-face session.

Classroom management strategies can—and should—be used as preventive measures. Weinstein (1996) assumes that "most problems of disorder in classrooms can be avoided if teachers use good preventive management strategies" (p. 6). This shifts the focus away from discipline to engaging students in activities. Once that is accomplished, students are poised to excel both in academics and character.

Conflict Resolution

What is conflict resolution? Conflict-resolution strategies incorporate skills that enable people to solve problems and avoid conflicts. Gordon's (1974) "NO-lose problem solving method" is one of the best-known and well-researched conflict-resolution methods. The six problem-solving steps are:

Step 1. Define the problem.

Step 2. Brainstorm possible solutions.

Step 3. Evaluate the solutions.

Step 4. Decide on a solution to try.

Step 5. Determine how to implement the decision.

Step 6. Evaluate the solution.

The goals of most programs are to resolve conflict and improve relations among people at the school level and in the larger community.

Why should you consider implementing a conflict-resolution program in your classroom or school? Schools are full of unresolved conflicts, which are the source of discipline problems, vandalism, and even violence. Often, these conflicts are resolved by external authority figures taking punitive disciplinary measures. These may succeed temporarily but do not resolve the source of the conflict. Conflict-resolution programs enable students to develop skills for resolving conflicts effectively, fostering self-discipline and leading to internally based control.

The benefits of conflict-resolution skills carry over into all aspects of life in school, at home, and in the community. The most obvious benefit is that the climate of the classroom and school improves dramatically. We conducted a review of the benefits of conflict-resolution programs by examining the literature and claims made by program proponents. We found that the outcomes expected for conflict-resolution and peer-mediation programs match up with many of the expectations for character education programs. Some of the major benefits of conflict-resolution programs are to

∾ Increase students' self-esteem

∾ Promote the appreciation of diversity

   🍠 Improve students' communication and analytical skills

   🍠 Prevent the escalation of disciplinary programs

   🍠 Improve communication among students, faculty, and administrators

   🍠 Increase the willingness and ability to solve conflicts among staff, students, and parents

   🍠 Develop cooperative relationships between the school and parents in resolving students' school problems

The benefits of any type of conflict-resolution program far outweigh the time and training factors required to implement it. We recommend that you look into one of the three types of conflict-resolution programs to see which type fits your current needs: (a) in-class model (mediation skills taught at the classroom level), (b) all-school model (program implemented schoolwide), and (c) law-related model (skills taught in the context of our judicial system, e.g., a school court or council).

Cooperative Learning

Many teachers implement group work, but few engage students in cooperative learning. So, what is cooperative learning? Cooperative learning engages the learner in meaningful and relevant tasks that require collaboration and group cooperation to complete an assignment. There are three essential elements of cooperative learning: task interdependence, role interdependence, and reward interdependence. Cooperative learning contexts provide a setting for creating a community of learners and practicing conflict-resolution skills. Current research on the effectiveness of cooperative learning indicates that when students work cooperatively, they are more attentive and on-task, they learn more and retention is higher, and they learn about group dynamics and develop positive interpersonal skills and prosocial values.

A review of Johnson, Johnson, Holubec, and Roy's (1984) book on cooperative learning suggests that there are links to instructional strategies that promote character. According to these authors, activities that include all three essential elements of cooperative learning will enable students to

- Reach higher levels of achievement
- Develop greater competencies in
  - ☑ Critical thinking
  - ☑ Attitude toward subjects
  - ☑ Working collaboratively
- Achieve greater psychological health
- Perceive grading as "fair"

Cooperative learning promotes

- Positive relationships
- Acceptance among students
- Higher levels of self-esteem
- Greater cognitive and affective perspective taking (vs. egocentrism)

Why don't more teachers use cooperative learning strategies in their classrooms? We can only assume that the time required to create interdependent tasks and the skills necessary to maintain appropriate individual and group rewards block teachers from implementing this highly effective strategy. Passive techniques, such as talking or reading about cooperative learning, are not effective methods for learning how to use this strategy. We recommend that teachers immerse themselves in workshops that model effective cooperative learning strategies so that they can experience the process while learning the skills and techniques to apply in their classrooms.

Citizenship

Character education programs can bring focus to the citizenship side of students' report cards. Civic education is an important component of a school's character education efforts. Murphy (1998) says that "A character-building citizenship program emphasizes the development of specific 'democratic' qualities such as justice, respect, fairness, cooperation, persistence, moral responsibility, empathy, and caring" (p. 178). Such programs should help students develop an awareness of the purpose and meaning of citizenship; an appreciation of life in a democratic society; the ability to analyze what works and what needs attention in governmental, group, and individual behaviors; and motivation to take action for the common good. Kirschenbaum (1995) suggests that citizenship education should require instruction in the knowledge of historical and current affairs, an appreciation of the American democratic system, as well as a recognition of its flaws and its shames. It should also require communication skills, cooperation skills, and conflict-resolution skills (including attention to peace education). Vessels (1998) has written citizenship behavioral objectives for students in grades 1 and 2, 3 to 5, and 9 to 12.

Award-winning schools (Murphy, 1998) offer citizenship programs that include a "buddy" program, citizenship awards, school and community-service projects, school patrols and scouts, students councils and clubs, and tutorial and sister-school programs. Some schools have implemented the CIVITAS curriculum in their schools; others structure the academic side of citizenship in their social studies curriculum.

There are several organizations that focus their attention on citizenship education, including the Center for Civic Education, the Association of Teacher Educators' National Commission on Democratic Practices in Education, and the Citizenship and Law Related Education Center (see Resources).

Critical Thinking

What is critical thinking? The basic principle is that you, as the teacher, can help create conditions that assist students in learning to be critical thinkers, problem solvers, and decision makers—all prerequisites to moral behavior. Ethical and moral decision making can help students reach the highest stage in Bloom's Taxonomy of Educational Objectives: the evaluation stage.

One example of critical thinking that can be applied across subject areas is the Socratic seminar. One primary goal of a Socratic seminar is that students will demonstrate their understanding of the ideas, values, and issues generated from any primary-source material by examining its validity. "This classical technique leads students to recognize contradictions between values they avow and the choices they make—and shows them that they have the power to choose" (Elkind & Sweet, 1997, p. 56). Socratic seminars create environments that engage students in participating in in-depth analyses of primary-source materials through questioning and enables them to apply evaluation skills.

Why should you use critical-thinking strategies? Researchers and practitioners have been advocating that we should help students learn "how to use their minds well" and develop "deep understandings" about content—rather than surface knowledge of facts—to understand multiple perspectives and to solve problems. Strategies such as Socratic seminars meet the expected outcomes of character education programs in that they help students develop "habits of mind" that model the thoughtful problem-solving strategies that most modern employers seek in new employees. Socratic seminars and other critical-thinking strategies help students make decisions for themselves and teach them how to make good choices and solve problems nonviolently. This, in effect, educates for character (Elkind & Sweet, 1997).

Critical thinking should be coupled with the other four classroom strategies. All five strategies, used in combination, will help teachers foster the consensus values of the community and increase students' academic achievement.

STAFF DEVELOPMENT

Staff development is an essential ingredient for success in implementing character education programs. Staff development must be appropriate, motivating, and informative; it must lead to helping teachers implement new techniques. Over the years, we have used and shared a variety of methods for adult staff development that are very effective. Some of these training methods are

    ☑ Case studies
    ☑ Role plays

☑ Simulations

☑ Socratic seminars

☑ Ethical analysis

☑ Videos and CD-ROMs

☑ Hands-on materials review

We recommend that you use some of these methods to help educators learn new information in meaningful, long-lasting ways. We discovered, in workshops, academies, and courses, that when we use the training methods listed above and model the practices teachers will use with their students, they understand how they can apply the methodology in their classrooms. Just talking about these strategies and methods does not work.

Staff development is necessary to ensure the success and longevity of character education programs. Using the recommended methods, you should plan to provide ongoing training for faculty in a variety of areas, depending on your areas of need. Your character education council can—and should— provide training for stakeholders in all the following areas:

- Consensus building

- Assessment—customizing instruments

- Action plans—community, school, classroom

- Implementing standards

- Curriculum development or adoption

- Classroom strategies

- Materials and programs—customizing use

- Resources—access and referral

CONCLUDING COMMENTS

Training is essential. Training is fundamental. Training can guarantee success of character education programs. Those programs that fail are likely to have either neglected the training of stakeholders or not sustained that training and support over time. The instructional strategies reported in this chapter have been found to be very effective in character education. These strategies should be taught to teachers in staff-development workshops, along with ongoing assistance, support, and access to resources provided in the implementation plan for the character education program. Teachers hold the key to success in character education programs, and we need to ensure that the strategies they implement are ones that will get the job done. The effective training methods listed in this chapter can be used to teach those instructional strategies.

QUOTES:
Something to Think About

I know of no research that shows a direct connection between values and behavior. Conversely, lots of research shows there is none. . . . I hope you will clarify your view before the erroneous assumption that teaching moral values will produce significant reductions in irresponsible behavior spreads.

—Lockwood, A. L. (1993). A letter to character educators.
Educational Leadership, 51(3), p. 73.

We know that character education works both from the formal evaluations and assessments that have been made . . . and from the enthusiastic testimony of parents, teachers, principals, and superintendents in districts where character education has been introduced in a serious way. It also stands to reason and common sense that students will behave better if they are provided strong, positive, consistent guidance on such character traits as respect, responsibility, honesty, and caring than if they are left completely on their own.

—The Character Education Partnership. Character Education:
Questions and Answers. Mimeograph, p. 4.

If we are to reach real peace in this world, and if we are to carry on a real war against war, we shall have to begin with the children.

—Mahatma Gandhi

QUESTIONS:
Something to Talk About

1. What are your questions about the major findings reported in this chapter?

2. How would you respond to the authors of the quotes above?

3. In your opinion, should we slow down character education efforts until more research gives us some definitive answers about the outcomes of such efforts?

4. How would you use the information in this chapter to help provide quality character education training in effective instructional methods in your school?

5. What additional information would you need to make a better case for the need for training and staff development to ensure the success of character education programs?

BOOKS:
Something to Read About

Kirschenbaum, H. (1995). *100 ways to enhance values and morality in school and youth settings.* Boston: Allyn & Bacon.

Leming, J. S. (1993). *Character education: Lessons from the past, models for the future.* Camden, ME: Institute for Global Ethics.

Ryan, K. & Bohlin, K. (1999). *Building character in schools.* San Francisco: Jossey-Bass.

Sizer, T. R., & Sizer, N. F. (1999). *The students are watching: Schools and the moral contract.* Boston: Beacon.

PROGRAMS:
Something to Investigate

Community of Caring

Program: Community of Caring (COC) works to implement and encourage five values—caring, responsibility, respect, trust, and family—in our nation's schools. By doing so, COC addresses destructive attitudes that lead to early sexual involvement, teen pregnancy, substance abuse, and dropping out of school. Through training for teachers, values discussions, teen forums, parent involvement, and community service, the COC addresses destructive attitudes that lead to early sexual involvement, teen pregnancy, substance abuse, delinquent behavior, and dropping out of school. COC research indicates a strong link between mental retardation and teen pregnancy. This program is an effort to prevent teen pregnancy and lower the incidence of mental retardation.

The COC is not a curriculum; it is an interactive process of questions, thoughts, reactions, and discoveries woven into an existing curriculum. Teachers learn to incorporate values discussions into textbook materials, athletics, and everyday school activities. The five values are articulated and demonstrated in relation to real-life, tough situations where students develop an understanding of how the values affect life choices and behavior. Through a total community approach, this program creates a caring, respectful school environment that supports students as they develop positive values. The school family, parents, and the community work together. Students accept responsibility for themselves and their future and grow toward adulthood with a clear sense of purpose, motivated by an understanding of the community good.

Results: The COC builds confidence, decision-making skills, responsibility, and a commitment to values. Teens make decisions that strengthen family relationships and encourage caring, and they experience a greater sense of confidence and self-worth. In addition, their academic performance improves. Incidences of teenage pregnancy, substance abuse, and truancy decrease, while the drop-out rate declines. Evaluations of this program support the "whole school, whole community" approach as more successful than topical programs designed as modules. For example, (a) students in three COC schools raised their grade point averages 43%, 46%, and 71%, respectively; (b) COC schools report reduced pregnancies; (c) COC students show greater gains in knowledge about the adverse consequences and risks of early sexual activity; (d) COC "high-risk" students were significantly more likely to plan postponing sex until after high school; and (e) COC students had fewer unexcused absences and, in general, fewer written disciplinary actions.

Contact: Community of Caring, 1325 G Street, NW, Washington, DC 20005; Tel: (202) 393-1251; Fax: (202) 824-0351.

Global Ethics

Program: The Institute for Global Ethics is dedicated to elevating public awareness and promoting the discussion of ethics in a global context. As an international, membership-based think tank, it focuses on ethical activities in education, the corporate sector, and public policy. The institute's mission is to (a) discover and articulate the global common ground of ethical values, (b) analyze ethical trends and shifts in values as they occur worldwide, (c) gather and disseminate information on global ethics, and (d) elevate public awareness and discussion of global ethical issues. It has developed curricular materials for use in K–12 settings, and its two-phase community-based character-education program equips teachers with the classroom materials and training needed to carry the program forward. One- or two-day seminar sessions for teachers train them to implement ethics into the daily curriculum, using "building decision skills" (BDS).

Results: The results of the BDS materials include qualitative comments from teachers, as well as some research results from a Kellogg-funded ethics and service-learning grant. Some typical teacher comments include

- "I love the whole program because it's really concise, it makes sense, and it's not too overwhelming."

- "I think it's a very good, concrete curriculum. It's not burdensome and it is very user-friendly."

◦ "It gives the teacher a springboard and that's primarily what we need. It doesn't take a lot of extra work to implement."

Research involving students showed that those who completed the program, compared to students who did not, ranked the values of honesty, community, and responsibility higher on a posttest. It was also found that the students who completed the BDS program were better able to interpret situations as having an ethical dimension and were better able to frame situations as a "right vs. right conflict," which is one of the program's main emphases.

Contact: Institute for Global Etics, 11 Main Street, PO Box 563, Camden, ME 04843; Tel: (207) 236-6658; Fax: (207) 236-4014.

CHAPTER 5

✥✥✥

Building Effective Home, School, and Community Partnerships

By the year 2000, every school will provide partnerships that will increase parent involvement and participation in promoting the social, emotional, and academic growth of children.

—National Educational Goals 2000

It is safe to say that now and in the future, it will take a community to raise a child. Parents (guardians and caregiving adults) are a child's first teachers and moral educators. Some are better than others. Some need help, others don't. Some know where to find help when they need it, but others are unaware of the resources available in the community. Most parents, as most of the public, believe that schools should participate in the moral development of the young. Most believe the schools need to teach values and prosocial behaviors to help combat the negative messages that their children learn from the media, malls, and models. This framework calls all community organizations to work to empower parents, to involve parents, and to support parents through a multiplicity of partnerships and services including:

- Schools
- Faith communities
- Health/social organizations
- Businesses
- Law enforcement and judicial groups
- Family outreach centers
- The media

We believe that school personnel, in particular, have a specific role to play in partnership programs designed to foster values and character. First, they need to help parents raise their children, help them network with other parents, and help them learn how best to find and use community resources. Second, they must prepare the next generation of parents—those young people in middle and secondary school—to learn about the meanings and responsibilities of being a parent; they need to be taught effective parenting skills and practices. Third, educators have to exert extraordinary efforts to bring parents, school personnel, and community service providers together. Fourth, they, along with parents and the community, must engage students in learning and practicing the consensus values. Partnerships should strengthen academic achievement and nurture personal and civic values.

THE CONCERN

According to David A. Hamburg (1991), President of the Carnegie Corporation, "Children are in crisis because families are in crisis" (p. 4). Joel Orosz (1995), in his analysis of the work of several social critics, says that "these authors agree that economic and emotional rootlessness, cultural tribalism, and rampant individualism have cumulatively had the effect of seriously damaging America's fami-

lies and neighborhoods" (p. 7). High rates of divorce and remar-
riages have required children to adjust to complex relationships.
Thousands of children are being born to teenagers. The two-parent
working family has resulted in much less interaction with children
(Hamburg, 1991).

Children are spending much more of their time out of their
homes. Some are in child care facilities and others are latchkey kids
with little adult supervision. Some children are in gangs and cliques
where they look for advice, counsel, and support. Television has
become the nation's babysitter. Recent reports indicate that although
the overall crime rate appears to be declining, there is a fear that
juvenile crime will continue to increase and become more violent
and random. As we write this book, new findings indicate that drug
use among teens is higher than predicted and is rising. Some states
are passing laws holding parents responsible for children's unlawful
behavior.

Americans have an uncanny knack to respond to crisis. The call
has gone out to citizens to re-create a culture of democratic values to
assist parents and guardians in the intellectual and moral development of their children. There are many families that are raising
young people to be productive, intelligent, and moral. These families come from all socioeconomic levels, all cultures, and all races.
But citizens also recognize that, given the conditions of modern family life, all families need support and assistance from their communities and schools.

The importance of community is eloquently expressed by
Gardner (1990) in a discussion about the functions of community.
He reminds us that the community is a "generator of value systems."
Other important functions of the community, says Gardner, are that
it should maintain, nurture, and foster support, trust, cooperation,
respect, and integrity among its members. The community should
be "an instrument for the accomplishment of group purpose" based
on a "philosophy of pluralism, an open climate for dissent," and a
relentless intent to eradicate discrimination. He points out that a
community can build coalitions, enhance members' performance
and motivations, assist diverse groups to come to know one another,
and provide opportunities to engage in conflict resolution, negotia-
tion, and mediation (pp. 4-5).

This is what the concern is all about—connecting citizens of all ages to their community, creating change to rebuild the concept of community, designing ways that the community can discuss and decide on its values, and creating a community culture of caring.

PARENT INVOLVEMENT

Character education participants should know that parent involvement in the education of their children positively influences their academic achievement and attitudes. Studies have shown that when parents are involved in the school, children get better grades, have more positive attitudes toward school and work, have higher expectations, and may exhibit more positive behaviors. For example, research by Henderson and Berla (1994) found that, first, when parents are able to play a variety of roles in their children's learning, their children do better. Second, they found that higher student achievement results when the family-school relation is comprehensive, well planned, and involves differing roles for parents. And third, they found that the best results for student achievement occur when families, community organizations, and schools work together. Studies also show that parent involvement decreases as children progress through the grades (at the middle and high school levels particularly) unless schools take extraordinary efforts to maintain involvement.

What, then, are the implications for character education? Will parent involvement in the character education program influence their children's behaviors? Will parent involvement in the school's efforts to foster the values of respect, for example, result in having more students demonstrate this value? Can we assume that parent involvement in promoting the value of honesty will influence their children's demonstration of that value? Appropriate questions but, to date, no definitive answers. It is our opinion (and, we think, just plain common sense) that parental involvement in school programs is essential both to the child and to the adults in that child's life. Can you imagine a character education program without parental involvement?

There are many federal, state, and local initiatives to involve parents in the education of their children. Knowledge of these initiatives is important to those who want to promote character education efforts in their schools and communities. Comprehensive parent involvement, according to a California policy, is illustrative and suggests that parents assume a variety of roles at all grade levels. Accordingly, school programs should be designed to

- Enhance parenting skills

- Establish conditions that support learning at home

- Assist parents in helping their children learn at home

- Coordinate community and support services for children and families

- Train parents so that they can become involved in the instructional and support services offered in school

- Communicate effectively and regularly with parents regarding school programs and their children's progress

- Assist parents in developing leadership and decision-making skills so that they can participate in governing, advocacy, and advising roles (Solomon, 1991).

The implications for leaders and for stakeholders in a school's character education program are obvious and should not be overlooked.

A PARTNERSHIP FRAMEWORK

As Ernest Boyer (1995) pointed out, "it's not the school that's failed, it's the partnership that's failed, with schools taking on responsibilities that families and communities and religious institutions once assumed" (p. 49). So how do schools, families, and community groups forge stronger, more meaningful partnerships?

We have recommended various organizational patterns to accomplish the work that needs to be done for creating, implementing, sustaining, and evaluating a comprehensive character education program. The organizational dilemma is this—should the community's character education efforts be independent of or a part of a school's district or a school's existing community partnership program? For example, most school districts have school partnership programs with a district coordinator and office staff. Should the district's character education program be a function of that office? Other schools have school site partnership committees. Should they take on the responsibilities of character education? Finally, some school districts or school sites have neither; there is no formal school council responsible for partnership efforts. Is there a best way to organize for partnership programs that would include character education?

The answer is—we don't know. But we think not! School districts and individual schools across this country vary to such a great extent that to suggest one best way to organize would be foolhardy. However, for purposes of illustration and discussion, we will continue our focus on the school site. Consequently, we will address our comments about the partnership framework to school site personnel, knowing that much of what we say is applicable in most instances to other school or community organizational arrangements.

The plan that we will outline in this chapter is based on an article by one of the eminent authorities on school, family, and community partnerships, Joyce Epstein. In this article, which should be read by all character development educators, Epstein (1995) proposes that each school create an action team. A summary of her planning outline follows.

Step 1: The Action Team for School, Family, and Community Partnerships

Membership. Three teachers and parents from different grade levels; one administrator and other school personnel; one member from the community; and at the middle and high school levels, at least two students from different grade levels. All members should be appointed to 2- to 3-year terms.

Subcommittees. Members of the action team elect the chair or co-chairs (or take on the assignment) for six subcommittees, one for each kind of involvement that is described in the "Epstein model"—

parenting, communicating, volunteering, learning at home, decision making, and collaborating with the community.

Responsibilities. Assess present practices, organize options for new partnerships, implement selected activities, evaluate next steps, and improve and coordinate practices for six kinds of involvement.

Step 2: Funding and Other Support

Epstein (1995) suggests funding from federal and state initiatives that require and recommend family support (about $1000 per year for use by the action team). Such resources would be used for staff development, demonstration program implementation, materials, other partnership expenses, time to do its work, and social support (p. 708).

Step 3: Identify Starting Points

The action team assesses current partnership practices and, using a variety of methods, solicits the "views, experiences, and wishes of teachers, parents, administrators, and students." The questions would center on such themes as existing strengths, needed changes, expectations, sense of community, and ties to specific school goals (Epstein, 1995, pp. 708-709).

Step 4: Develop a 3-Year Plan

Suggestions include developing a comprehensive 1-year plan and outlining the work of each subcommittee over the 3 years. This plan should include specific activities, create a monthly action timeline, identify personnel responsible for implementation of each activity, and should be shared by all participants. The action team addresses "details, responsibilities, costs, and evaluation" (Epstein, 1995, p. 709).

Step 5: Continue Planning and Working

Suggestions include updating the 3-year plan, developing a detailed 1-year plan, scheduling annual presentations, arranging an annual conference, arranging for celebration of progress, working for yearly improvement, exploring new opportunities, thinking about partnership as a "process, not a single event," connecting programs and activities to curricular and instructional reform, and redefining staff development "to mean colleagues working together and with parents to develop, implement, evaluate, and continue to improve practices of partnership" (Epstein, 1995, pp. 709-710).

We repeat, our purpose for presenting the Epstein model is to encourage character educators to create meaningful and lasting partnerships with families and the community.

CHARACTER EDUCATION PARTNERSHIP ACTION TEAM (PAT)

We took Epstein's idea, modified it, and created a framework for a school site partnership action team that includes a Partnership Action Team (PAT) and a Character Education Evaluation Committee (CEEC). (The CEEC is highlighted and discussed in Chapter 6.)

PAT's objective. To build effective and efficient character education partnerships with the school's parents and the school's immediate or surrounding community so that the goals of the character education program are supported.

PAT's membership. Membership will vary depending on the size of the school and the outside organizations that become involved. Representatives from each of the organizations may be on the team, or if the group is too large, subcommittees can be formed and made part of the framework.

PAT's support. The team examines all possibilities for financial and other resources and creates a budget plan for the first 3 years; most "low-cost" activities may be implemented as planned; "high-cost" activities should wait until funded.

PAT's plans. The first task for the team is to address the partnership standards (see below) and to plan an array of partnership activities for school personnel, for parents, and for community leaders that put the standards in action. The character education program and the consensus values are implemented through special programs (after-school programs, service learning programs, life skills programs), through a family outreach center, through prevention programs (drug, alcohol, accident), through special school activities and events, and through the existing curriculum.

PAT's assessment. The team works with the school's CEEC to plan and implement assessment activities based on the partnership standards. For example, in Chapter 6, a parent questionnaire on the effectiveness of the school's character education program can be used by the CEEC to inform the PAT about parental perceptions about the program.

PARTNERSHIP STANDARDS

To highlight the importance of character education partnerships, we propose the following standards.

Standard 1

The school character education efforts must be in close concert with parents. Forming effective partnerships is essential to the success of any character education program.

Standard 2

Parents, guardians, and child care providers should be active participants in character education program planning and evaluation, particularly in the school(s) that their children attend.

Standard 3

A community's character education program will provide parents and homes with "full-service" opportunities to help meet students' physical, social, and emotional needs.

Standard 4

All school personnel need skills and strategies to assist parents in helping their children become successful learners, and to help parents cope with typical and atypical problems of raising children.

Standard 5

Because research shows a drop-off in parental involvement as children progress through the grades, school personnel in middle and high schools must make special efforts to maintain parental interest in and involvement with the schools to help foster character education efforts (NASSP, 1996).

Standard 6

The community agencies and businesses are equally important and can do a great deal to help parents become involved in the cognitive and moral development of their children.

Standard 7

School personnel must *care* about parental involvement; they must *communicate* frequently and effectively with parents; they must value *collaboration* and create ways to enhance it; they must have a *coherent* plan of action; and they must be willing to *change* those factors that detract from the creation of effective home, school, and community partnerships.

The next section presents some ideas for the PAT to consider when implementing changes that would strengthen partnerships while serving the objectives and purposes of the school's character education efforts. Effective partnerships need organization. We focus on a school site organizational plan, recognizing that many school districts will have a central office that promotes, implements, and monitors partnership programs for the district. But as we have said before, the relationships usually take place at the school site where parents send their children because that's where the partnerships begin and end; that's where the community comes together to create a caring environment, to foster the values, to provide services, and to support one another's efforts. So for the local school site partnership action team, we offer the following A-Z ideas and suggestions.

ABC'S FOR THE SCHOOL'S CHARACTER EDUCATION PARTNERSHIPS

A. Acceptance

Schools, according to many experts, are not good at creating partnerships with parents and others. The PAT needs to prepare all school personnel to accept parents and community members as partners in the school's character education program. It just won't happen without training, new perspectives, and expectations about what partnerships can be. For example, some school personnel may see parents as detractors, or they may have low expectations of parent support and resources. But the reality is that the time is long gone when a school can tell parents, "Send us your children and we will educate them."

B. Barriers

There are several barriers to effective partnerships, and most should be thoroughly explored in the PAT's planned inservice programs. A few areas that may present barriers include language, socioeconomic level, culture, work schedule of parents, time, and transportation. Special attention in all communication about the school's character education program should be given to parents and community members who use English as a second language. The PAT should ensure that planning for school programs and activities, from conferences to competitions to celebrations, take into account each of the potential barriers.

C. Communication

Research shows that when parents receive frequent and effective communication from teachers,

- ∽ Their level of involvement in their children's learning increases.

- ∽ Children are more positive in their perceptions of their parents' level of involvement, in their attitudes toward parental involvement, and in their motivation to learn.

- ∽ Teachers who believe in their ability to involve parents initiate more communication with parents.

- ∽ Parents who believe in their ability to influence their children's success report greater involvement in their children's learning

- ∽ It has a significant affect on parents' overall evaluations of the teacher and their feelings of comfort with the school. (Hollifield, 1995)

The results of clear, continuous, and meaningful communication with parents influence students' academic achievement and may have implications for character education efforts as well. It is information such as this that should be examined by the team and others during inservice character education workshops and seminars.

D. Discipline

Books, articles, and programs on school discipline proliferate the education literature. It is not our intention here to add to the excellent information that is available on the topic. Our intention is, however, to alert the team to the relationship between discipline policies and practices and the character education program. We offer a short discipline checklist and then pose some questions.

☑ The school has a written code of rules and regulations for students.

☑ The discipline code clearly delineates the consequences for types of misbehaviors.

☑ Discipline policies and procedures are published and widely disseminated.

☑ Students and parents sign pledges to support the policies and procedures.

☑ Teachers have classroom meetings to discuss the discipline code with students and solicit student input.

☑ The discipline policies and procedures foster self-discipline, self-respect, responsibility, and other values in the school's character education program.

☑ Teaching strategies are used to help students think before they act and to prevent problems before they occur.

☑ In each classroom, behavioral expectations are clear, consistent among teachers, and connected to school policies.

☑ Discipline policies and procedures include expected behaviors outside the classroom—on the bus, in corridors and restrooms, in the media center, and in cocurricular programs.

☑ The policies and practices are reviewed annually.

The team may pose the following questions to school personnel as part of the character education efforts:

- How does the way we handle discipline in this school contribute to the objectives of the character education program?

- Are the discipline policies and practices aligned with the values that we are trying to foster?

- Have we effectively involved students and parents in developing and implementing our discipline policies and practices?

- Are our discipline practices promoting the values inherent in self-discipline, self-reliance, self-esteem, and respect for others?

 ᴥ Have we adequately prepared school personnel and parents to use methods that help students examine their behaviors and take responsibility for their actions?

 ᴥ Has the character education program had any recognizable effect on the discipline problems we have had at this school?

E. Emotion and Empathy

In the popular best-seller by Daniel Goleman (1996), *Emotional Intelligence,* the author says that

> in a time when too many children lack the capacity to handle their upsets, to listen or focus, to rein in impulse, to feel responsible for their work or care about learning, anything that will buttress these skills will help in their education. In this sense, emotional literacy enhances the schools' ability to teach. . . . There is an old fashioned word for the body of skills that emotional intelligence represents: *character.* (pp. 384-385)

Thomas Lickona (1991) reminds us that emotions have a major, but overlooked, role in the character development of children and youth. Lickona says the emotional side of our moral selves that should be developed at home and school is captured in such words as *conscience, self-esteem, empathy, loving the good,* and *humility* (pp. 56-61). Our experiences and observations, like yours no doubt, clearly suggest that emotions can and do interfere with rational decision making.

Empathy training, learning to "put oneself in the shoes of another," conducted in several elementary schools (with 8- to 10-year-olds) has shown that students who participated in the training were less aggressive, had a more positive self-concept, and showed more prosocial behaviors than students who did not participate in the training (Hamburg, 1994). We suggest that the team consider emotional and empathy training for students and parents as part of the character education program.

F. Families

The PAT has to find ways for families to foster the consensus values of the character education program in their homes. The case has been made in this book and elsewhere for the importance of families as character educators and the need for schools and the community to assist parents in raising their children. The team can enhance partnerships with families when school personnel and particularly school leaders do the following:

- Really know each of the families in the school.
- Establish policies and procedures that involve and support families.
- Promote practices that respond to family needs, interests, questions, talents.
- Establish a community team effort to develop partnerships with families.
- Impress on school personnel the need for effective communication with families.
- Provide family opportunities to use the school for education, recreation, social, and health services.
- Encourage students to help promote the values of family life.
- Encourage all participants to suggest better ways to involve families in school affairs.
- Help families learn about and practice the program's values at home.
- Examine the effectiveness of character education materials sent to and used by families.
- Periodically evaluate efforts to assess family-school-community relationships. (Henderson & Berla, 1994)

G. Grouping Students

There are a variety of ways to group students for academic and character education purposes such as skill groups, remedial groups, peer teaching groups, special interest groups, project groups, independent study groups, service learning groups—all under the umbrella of cooperative learning. The instructional and social benefits of effective group strategies in classrooms and schools are many. It is in groups that students learn interpersonal relationship skills, enhance their self-esteem, become motivated to learn, learn to be responsible, learn how to compromise, problem solve, make decisions, and discover the values of sharing and caring. We add grouping students to PAT's tasks because we believe it remains an untapped teaching strategy that attends to both the academic needs of students and to the objectives of the character education program. It needs greater use, continuing research, and support from parents.

H. Heroes and Heroines

Character education is about the study of persons, places, practices, perceptions, plans, pain, and pleasure. It is about learning from the experiences of heroes, heroines, villains, and vainglorious persons. Character education is learning about individuals and groups in the literature of the masses (newspapers, magazines, television) and the literature of the schools (science, music, literature, art, film, drama, social studies, and language arts courses). Our suggestion to the team is that they promote a values-based subject matter program for the school and homes that encompasses the study of heroes and heroines (see the Giraffe Project example in Chapter 2). We provide no set formula for doing this. Our intent is to alert you to the richness found in the fictional and actual lives of people. Whether in print, on the stage, or on film, the hearts and minds of children and youth can be engaged by heroes and heroines. There are lessons to be learned, hearts to be moved, and imaginations to be stimulated.

I. Invite, Inform, Involve

One of the PAT's first tasks is to find effective ways to invite parents to participate in their children's learning, be it academic, social, or personal. Following this invitation, parents need to be informed about the school's character education initiatives and the values to be fostered in that program. They need to know what the program is all about, why it is necessary, and what their role is to be. Then they need genuine invitations and options for involvement. We know we are stating the obvious. We know we are being repetitive. We know that parent involvement is not easy, given the pressures on parents' time, energy, and resources. We also know that without parent involvement in the character education program, the chances for success are greatly diminished.

J. Joe, Jack, Julio, Jason

All masculine names and our way of reminding the partnership teams that they may have to pay special attention to males, men, fathers, and stepfathers. Many children lack male role models. Many children see their fathers on an irregular basis, if at all. Some children wonder who their fathers are and where they are. The decline of fatherhood, the increased divorce rate, and the absence of fathers from the home for whatever reason rob from the young the benefits of interacting personally and intimately with males and learning what it means to be male. How much this trend of separation has contributed to youth problems and other data reported in Chapter 1 is anyone's guess. Our suggestion to the PAT is that, within the character education program, it give special attention to engaging all students in the study of fatherhood and also that special efforts be made to involve fathers and men in all aspects of the program.

K. Knowledge of Families and Community

Ernest Boyer (1995) suggests that schools create an inventory of parent skills and experiences and find out the kinds of volunteer work that parents would like to do. We want to add to this suggestion. All school personnel should know the community "movers," and know where and how to access and use community resources. This begins when the team develops a computerized data bank of people and places, organizations and groups. It begins with school personnel—their contacts, their memberships in civic or charitable groups, and an inventory of their knowledge of the community.

The data bank might also include information about civic organizations, colleges and universities, proprietary and other schools, recreational facilities, volunteer groups, media and businesspeople, clubs (both social and civic), community leaders, law enforcement offices, health agencies, graduates of the school, and businesses near the school, as well as parks, museums, art galleries, and religious institutions. If school personnel want to be a resource to parents, then they have to know the community. If they want to use the community to promote the academic and character education programs of the school, then they have to know the community. If they want to involve the community in promoting the consensus values and other aspects of the character education program, then they have to know the community.

L. *Love*

Well, we all know that love is a four-letter word. What we don't know is why people in the character education business don't talk about it more than they do. Maybe it is too elusive a value or considered too personal. Maybe we use it to cover a multitude of things from "I love you, man!" to "U.S.A.—Love it or leave it!" and by doing so, delimit its true meaning. Love is the tie that binds—parent to children, child to father and mother, sibling to sibling, and maybe even teacher to student. Thomas Lickona (1991) says that "love, like authority, is foundational" (p. 30). He also tells the story of a high school teacher whose reputation, teaching style, and relationships with students are "testimony to the power of treating students with love and respect" (pp. 72-73).

The Fresno (California) Unified School District is one of the few districts that lists love as one of its nine civic values and dedicates the month of December to feature this value. The district defines love as follows:

> Love is the supreme value. It is an emotion growing out of inner peace which follows a decision to act in response to the need of others. It involves a commitment to justice. It leads to subordination of personal desire in order to act with compassion in behalf of others. It is expressed as kindness, generosity, humility, unselfishness, loyalty, consideration, even-

temperedness and sincerity. It also involves a longing for the good, the true and the beautiful.[1]

We have no specific recommendations to PATs about the value of love except to say that it is an important, if often neglected, topic in character education programs.

M. Mentors

PATs may wish, through their "partnership office" to promote the character education program and its values by establishing a mentoring program. Parents could mentor other parents, college and high school students could mentor younger students, and community partners could engage in one-on-one mentoring, adult to child, arranged through the partnership office. Mentoring could be for personal development (including fostering the community values), career purposes, or educational reasons.

> There is a crucial need to help adolescents acquire durable self-esteem, reliable and relatively close human relationships, a sense of belonging in a valued group, and a sense of usefulness in some way beyond the self. Shaping these fundamental attributes in growth-promoting directions requires constructive models, mentors, and mediators. (Hamburg, 1986, p. 10)

N. Newspapers

Daily newspapers are filled with real-life examples of people facing moral dilemmas, fostering a value, and ignoring a value. There are heroes and villains, values-laden problems and events that are all told within articles, editorials, comics, and cartoons that can be used effectively in the instructional program. Also, there are daily newspapers actively engaged in their community's character education program.

One example is the cooperation between the Metropolitan Nashville Public Schools and the local newspaper, *The Tennessean*. The two organizations developed a program whose mission was to ensure that all students and parents, grades K–4, have the opportunity to experience an enhanced character education curriculum.

Each month during the school year, "Project Solution" distributes two tabloid-sized publications to students in grades K–4 that focus on these character education descriptors: respects self, does what is right, respects others, solves problems, accepts responsibility, builds community, cares, nurtures family members and friends, loves learning, takes initiative, models democratic ideals and practices, forgives, practices honesty, perseveres, demonstrates gratitude and courage, gives service, and respects work. Included in the program are staff development opportunities, a direct teaching approach emphasizing heroes of fiction and nonfiction, a role for parents with parent workshops, and a mentoring program using high school students as role models for the K–4 feeder schools.[2]

O. Opportunities

Opportunities to involve families and the community in the school's character education programs are limited only by the PAT's imagination and resources. The opportunities for a parent resource center—for children and youth to experience positive one-on-one interactions with adults, for home visits, for parent education, and for company employees to learn about and promote the values in their homes and at the workplace as their children are learning them at school—remain untapped. Opportunities abound for the community to decide how each organization, agency, and individual adult and student can best contribute to the goals of a school's character education program and the values that they wish students to learn and practice. The opportunities for students to learn the values as they engage in programs and services offered by the community in which they live are limited only by people's willingness to participate and by available resources.

P. Personal Reflection

One example of plans to find out how school personnel feel about parent involvement would require the team to create a questionnaire for teachers at the school site. The questionnaire would ask teachers to reflect on their feelings and attitudes about parent involvement in their classrooms and in the school as part of the character education program. Sample questions might include

1. What are my feelings about involving parents in my classroom?

2. How are my relationships with each of my students' parents?

3. How effective is my communication with parents?

4. How have I involved parents in fostering the values of our character education program?

5. How do I show students that I care about them and their families?

6. Have I asked parents to share with me or with the team their ideas on how best to promote the values of the program?

7. Have I talked with my students about their ideas for promoting the values at school, at home, and in the neighborhood?

8. Do I encourage students to reflect on the consensus values and to talk with their parents about the values being promoted at the school or the school's character education program?

9. Have I examined ways to integrate the values into the subjects I teach and then communicate that to students and their parents?

10. How can I do a better job involving and supporting parents' efforts to foster and nurture the values?

The team can use these questions to engage teachers and other school personnel in discussions about parent involvement, or it can use them as a survey to collect data on how teachers feel about parent involvement and practices.

Q. Questions for Community Organizations

The team, in the early phase of its work, should ask each community group to answer these questions and bring their responses to one of several meetings for discussion.

   √ What can your organization do to help promote the consensus values?

   √ What do you need to know about the school's character education program and what it is doing to foster these values?

   √ In what ways can your organization help parents/families promote the values?

   √ What should be the role that your organization assumes in the school's character education initiatives?

   √ What school programs and activities would best address your interests and gain your support?

   √ Is your organization willing to allow employees special benefits if they engage in the school's character education program?

   √ What services might your organization provide children and their parents/guardians who are from families in need?

R. Resource Room

One of the team's first tasks is to find space at school to create a room for resources and hire a partnership coordinator. This might be part of the effort to create and integrate school-based community services designed to provide social, health, mental health, and support services to meet the needs of children and their families. Or it could be an office where the coordinator and volunteers create a place for parents to meet, network, ask questions, and seek community resources. Open from 7:00 a.m. to 8:00 p.m., the resource room could arrange with the school librarian to have children's books available that emphasize values with characters who find themselves in moral dilemmas. It would have books for adults on a variety of topics about moral development and character education. The office would create a "talent bank" or Web site that catalogs the skills, hobbies, needs, interests, and experiences of parents and community members involved with the school. It would also have a database of all community and educational social service organizations that can be used by parents, teachers, and upper grade students. The office would promote programs that focus on the consensus values of the character education program.

S. Standards

Standards are the values of something established by general consent, such as the consensus values. They are targets to aim for, signposts to follow. We believe in standards: standards for student academic achievement; standards for student prosocial behaviors; standards for school programs; curriculum standards; teaching standards; and standards for community efforts to service children and youth.

In Chapter 2, we offered 15 program standards and implementation standards (the "11 C's"). In Chapter 3, we identified standards for a school's curriculum. In Chapter 4, we described seven teaching standards. In this chapter, we listed eight partnership standards. In Chapter 6, our list of 35 questions is intended to be used as a standards checklist for assessment. The team should revisit all of the standards within this book periodically throughout its work as a way of measuring the success and the quality of the character education program.

T. Television

The team must address how best to inform all partners in the school's character education initiatives about the adverse effects of television programming. It may be a window to the world, but it can also be a door to degradation of personal and civic values. Several educational organizations, in concert with medical, psychological, and sociological associations, have warned the public about the levels of violence on television, about how viewing this violence, day after day, can have a deleterious effect on children's and youth's behavior. More than two-thirds of the American public believe that television contributes to violence, crime, and an erosion of values. There is also evidence that students who watch a lot of television fail to do their homework and score lower on achievement tests.

In our opinion, most television is junk food for the brain and is filled with programming that lacks civility and taste. It is also a powerful educational medium, and when programs are carefully selected, the medium offers educationally rich and entertaining programs. We suggest that it is the PAT's responsibility, as part of the school's character education program, to harness the positive aspects of television and expose its tendencies to debase and defame. To do this, the PAT must create media literacy programs for students and their parents. It must help parents learn how best to monitor the television programs that their children watch. It needs to promote workshops and seminars for teachers and parents to inform them about television and the violence it portrays.

U. Uniforms

We were talking to a middle school teacher who told us that the change in her school and classroom environment when the school adopted uniforms last year was pleasantly surprising to all. She went on to talk about the changes in student attitudes toward school, learning, and one another. She also stated that the new uniform policy seemed to influence the teachers to dress more professionally.

Although there is controversy surrounding the use of uniforms and dress codes, there appear to be perceptions that they work in communities where uniforms and dress codes have been tried. For example, in Long Beach, California, one year after implementing the requirement that all students (K–8) wear uniforms, the district reports that fighting decreased 51%, weapon possession decreased 50%, assault and battery decreased 34%, vandalism decreased 18%, and suspension decreased 33% (Gursky, 1996). These are impressive results. The message may be, "Dress for success!" Or the idea at least raises the question, "Do the clothes make the student?" (Million, 1996, p. 5)

Uniforms and dress codes continue to be controversial in some communities. On one side, there is presidential endorsement of uniforms, and on the other, there is the ACLU's concerns about discrimination. In between, some inner-city youths claim that uniforms or dress codes make wearing gang colors a nonissue. Cause-and-effect relationships are difficult to substantiate based on the information to date, but there does appear to be enough interest in school uniforms to cause the U.S. Department of Education Safe and Drug Free

Schools Office (1996) to distribute a six-page manual of guidelines and model programs. The team may want to explore the possibility of requiring school uniforms. Or it may choose to ignore this suggestion on the grounds that is may cause community controversy that might detract from other character education efforts.

V. Violence

Violence prevention has to be part of any character education program. We have already talked about violence on television. It would seem impossible to foster values such as respect, responsibility, tolerance, and caring if the school is unsafe, and if the environment in and around school is such that children and young people are fearful of assaults, fights, stealing, name-calling, and drive-by shootings. Our intention here is not to offer solutions but to suggest that the team use community resources and design specific intervention programs to help community groups and schools make violence prevention and safety concerns part of the character education program.

We note that in January 1995, the Metropolitan Life Insurance Company ran full-page ads in several education journals that posed the question, "Can talk reduce school violence?" The ad reported that children who communicate with their families and parents are less likely to become victims of school violence. Children who are victims of violence feel isolated from responsible adults. This adult-student relationship (see Mentoring) was highlighted in an article about Huntington Beach High School, where teachers and staff created "personalization" strategies (e.g., adopt-a-kid program, violence prevention program, student forums, peer assistance leaders program) that were successful in curbing students' disruptive behaviors, improving the campus climate, raising test scores, and decreasing suspensions (Shore, 1996).

W. What's Working?

That is *the* question! After all is said and done, does character education change the behavior of students for the better? How does character education benefit the school, families, and community? What is the program worth to the school and the community? You can wait for answers or turn to the end of each chapter, where we provide findings from selected character education programs throughout the country. Each PAT can request that the character education evaluation committee (CEEC) find answers to these and "what's working" questions (see Programs: Something to Investigate at the end of each chapter.)

X. X-Factor

The "X-factor" is the unknown. Any change in an organization creates the X-factor, the fear of what might happen, good or bad. In character education programs, the X-factor may be the unanticipated results. It might be the surprises that result from promoting the values of the program. Or it might be concerns with program results. The X-factor may be comprehensive plans sacrificed for lack of resources. It may be events that the PAT did not plan for— challenges to the consensus values; concerns about program goals versus individual freedoms. The X-factor may be students' reactions to the program. Or it might be found in a statement by David Elkind (1995): "If our students are doing less well academically perhaps it is at least partly because our schools are devoting more of their resources to meeting the nonacademic needs of students" (p. 14).

At best, members of the team can plan; they can involve stakeholders; they can provide feedback; they can instruct; they can manage; and they can lead. But they cannot anticipate all of the X-factors because anything new, any change, will bring with it surprises, barriers, disappointments, challenges, and rewards.

Y. You

The character education efforts in communities and schools depend on you—individuals who care about youth; who care about families; who care about their community. You can and do make a difference!

Z. Zeitgeist

Zeitgeist is a German word meaning the spirit of the age, its intellectual, moral, and cultural climate. Let us hope that the zeitgeist of the 21st century will positively reflect the character and moral development efforts begun in the last two decades of the 20th century.

A FINAL WORD

In this chapter, we discussed the need for and importance of family-school-community partnerships. We suggested a framework for a school site where a Partnership Action Team takes the lead. We also proposed a list of partnership standards. In essence, the charge to character educators is to

- Create new ways to form effective, collaborative partnerships with parents and community organizations

- Become advocates and supporters of parents' efforts to raise their children

- Become initiators and catalysts for a values-based education

- Test the effectiveness of new and creative partnership efforts

- Find out about best practices and current research

- Examine policies, procedures, and practices that enhance or detract from sustained family-school-community partnerships

- Prepare parents and community groups for their roles and responsibilities in partnership programs, as well as in character education programs

The role for leaders in the character education program at each school is to incorporate the program into the current (and probably traditional) partnership programs, or to use the character education program to enhance partnerships that truly engage families and the community in the life of the school and in all of its programs and services. Either way, there is a need for strong partnerships between parents, schools and community agencies who can effectively collaborate and communicate with one another to show that they truly care about children and youth.

QUOTES:
Something to Think About

What needs to be different today in our conceptualizing the home/ school, parent/teacher relationship is a mutual realization that both are primary educators, both are directors of learning environments that shape the mind and heart of the child, and both are often in competition with other "teachers" such as the peer group, the media, and the like.

—Fantini, M., & Cardenas, R. (1980).
Parenting in a multicultural society.
New York: Longman, p. 211.

Rarely do schools acknowledge the power of peer culture in defining standards, and rarely do they take advantage of this power as an engine for quality. When students themselves are in charge of projects that they care about, peer pressure can become a powerful force for high standards.

—Berger, R. (1996).
Building a school culture where quality is "cool."
The Harvard Education Letter, 7(2), 5.

It is crucial that they [today's young people] be morally literate— possessed of a strong sense of right and wrong, a broad understanding of our culture's values, a foundation for making responsible decisions in the face of moral conflicts, and in general, a firm grasp of the rights and responsibilities of American citizenship.

—Heller, J. (1996).
Offering moral education.
Streamlined Seminar, 8(1), 1.

QUESTIONS:
Something to Talk About

1. How would you explain to parents and community leaders the need for a comprehensive character education program?

2. What are some of your ideas for involving parents in the affairs of the school and in the education of their children?

3. What information in this chapter caused you to examine your role for involving parents and community leaders in the school's character education efforts?

4. What strategies would you recommend that would help the people you work with pay greater attention to developing meaningful family-school-community partnerships?

5. How might you go about enhancing the relationship between the school and your community's social service agencies?

BOOKS:
Something to Read About

Child Development Project. (1994). *At home in our schools: A guide to school-wide activities that build community.* Oakland, CA: Developmental Studies Center.

Dotson, A., & Dotson, K. (1997). *Teaching character: Parents guide.* Chapel Hill, NC: Character Development Publishing.

Epstein, J., Coates, L., Salinas, K. C., Sanders, M. G., & Simon, B. S. (1997). *School, family, and community partnerships: Your handbook for action.* Thousand Oaks, CA: Corwin.

Legette, H. (1999). *Parents, kids, and character.* Chapel Hill, NC: Character Development Publishing.

Swap, S. (1993). *Developing home-school partnerships: From concepts to practice.* New York: Teachers College Press.

PROGRAMS:
Something to Investigate

Child Development Project (CDP)

Program: The Child Development Project (CDP) is an exemplary program with research to support its influence on elementary school teachers, students, parents, and the classroom climate. With permission, we have abstracted information provided by the CDP that addresses three questions.

What is the goal of CDP? To work with elementary schools to create stable, warm, and intellectually challenging environments where children can become thoughtful, knowledgeable, caring, principled, and self-disciplined.

What makes CDP unique? It focuses on an integrated approach to fostering children's ethical, social, and intellectual development. The program is based on the best available research and theory in education and child development, developed over 15 years, and has been rigorously evaluated.

What are the elements of CDP? The elements include a school-wide program to build community; a values-rich program of reading and language arts; cooperative learning strategies that build classroom community; classroom management that builds on personal responsibility and is based on respectful, caring relationships; and a parent involvement program that is simple and inclusive.

Results: CDP teachers were significantly more likely to provide opportunities for student autonomy and input; teach in ways that highlight prosocial values and promote social understanding; show warmth and supportiveness towards students; use forms of discipline that build students' personal commitment to responsible behavior; and use cooperative learning strategies. Students were significantly more likely to behave considerately, helpfully, and cooperatively in their classrooms; express greater motivation for learning and greater liking for school; score better on a measure of higher order reading comprehension; believe in the effectiveness of their personal efforts; resolve problems in ways that take all parties' needs into consideration. One or two years after leaving CDP schools, students (seventh and eight graders) were significantly more likely to score high on measures of conflict resolution skill and self-esteem; be involved in extracurricular activities; be rated by their teachers as assertive and popular; and have friends who were involved in positive activities (Viadero, 1994).

Contact: Eric Schaps, President, Developmental Studies Center, 2000 Embarcadero, Suite 305, Oakland, CA 94606-5300; Tel: (510) 533-0213.

NOTES

1. Correspondence from Marvin Awbrey, Social Science Coordinator, Fresno Unified School District, California.

2. For information contact Shirley D. McElroy, Project Solution Coordinator, *The Tennessean*, 1100 Broadway, Nashville, TN 37203.

CHAPTER 6

⋖⊙⊚⊙⋗

Assessing Your Character Education Programs

> *. . . The central function of schooling is to cultivate the mental and moral habits that a modern democracy requires.*
>
> —Deborah Meier

Previous chapters provided background information about character education, offered a framework that would help you and others implement and sustain a program, and discussed ways of involving the school, home, and community in the important work of character development. This chapter is about another component of the framework—evaluation. It focuses on ways of finding out who is responsible for evaluating a school's attempt to foster character development. This chapter is about documenting and tracking successes and failures. It is about saying, "This is what we are doing and why, and here is what we found and why." This chapter offers evaluation ideas, examples, guidelines, and suggestions.

The focus again is at the school site (with implications for a school district), where efforts to foster character education take place, where values are validated, where school personnel have a close relationship with students and their parents, where one needs to know what is working and what is not, and where character education will succeed or fail.

ORGANIZING FOR EVALUATION

The evaluation of a school's character education initiatives should be a collaborative effort among stakeholders. Evaluation should be an integral part of the program, should occur throughout the program with a timetable, and should be appropriately financed. Therefore, as we suggested in Chapter 5, each school should organize for assessment purposes by creating a character education evaluation committee (CEEC), which may be a subcommittee of the school's Character Education Council (see Chapter 5). This committee would be expected to carry out the following nine tasks.

Task 1

Membership on a school's CEEC should include teachers, administrators, other school personnel, staff, parents, community representatives, students, and perhaps an evaluation expert from the community, local college, or university. Membership size and composition will vary if the character education program is organized at the district or school level.

Task 2

The school's CEEC should spend time discussing purposes and responsibilities. This discussion might revolve around such questions as: Why has this committee been formed? What are our purposes? What are we expected to do? (See Step 3 in this chapter—Asking the Right Questions.)

Task 3

As the committee enters into discussions to answer these and other questions, it should consider the following evaluation guidelines.

- The evaluation plan should determine the extent to which the character education program's goals and objectives are being accomplished.

- The evaluation plan should not be one that tries to evaluate everything at once.

- The evaluation plan should accompany instructional and programmatic efforts so that the committee can provide stakeholders with current, ongoing information (Thomas, 1991).

- The evaluation plan should include a variety of assessment methods that will provide stakeholders with numerical data as well as deep, rich descriptions of events and relationships (Thomas, 1991).

- Evaluation methods should focus on ways to assess students' performance in knowing and demonstrating the consensus values fostered in the character education program.

- Evaluation plans should include ways to assess how students reflect on and think about values they hold and those they are learning in the school's character education program (Thomas, 1991).

- Evaluation efforts should contribute to program improvement, positive behavioral changes, and a caring school and classroom climate.

- The evaluation process itself should contribute to the value of self-appraisal, self-reflection, and self-education.

- The evaluation plan should provide school personnel with opportunities to diagnose difficulties, improve the existing program, and test new and creative projects or approaches.

- The evaluation process should be a team effort that brings together people who want to be held accountable for the program.

Task 4

The CEEC should study the research to find out how others are evaluating their character education programs. For example, Henry Huffman (1994), a former assistant superintendent of instruction, provides useful evaluation guidelines based on his experiences in a school district that created, implemented, and evaluated a character education program. He offers seven suggestions:

1. Evaluation should accompany program implementation.

2. School personnel need to review the character education research. Huffman cites the Child Development Project (see Programs at the end of this Chapter) as one that was of particular interest to the district's "Character Education Strategy Team" because it included a literature-based approach, a collaborative model, a caring approach to classroom management and discipline, and a plan for family involvement.

3. Evaluate the process of implementing the character education program so that problems can be corrected immediately.

4. A district's or school's current methods of evaluating student performance should not be altered by assessment methods used in the character education program. Huffman says that parents were informed that students would not be graded on a position they took on a controversial issue. He noted also that parents were informed that the current report card assessed such behaviors as courtesy, respect for others, respect for property, and observations of school rules and regulations.

5. Assessment plans begin with goals and use a variety of methods for collecting data, including journals, logs, anecdotes, self-reports, quantifiable information, perception surveys, checklists, tests, examinations, rating scales, questionnaires, polls, interviews, meetings, focus groups, and the like.

6. In the design and implementation of the evaluation phase of the character education program, it is important to involve all school personnel, parents, and students.

7. Create evaluation partnerships with local colleges and universities, educational agencies, and appropriate community agencies (pp. 75-82).

Task 5

The evaluation committee should determine what might be evaluated, when, where, and by whom. The committee should create a timeline. For example, the CEEC might decide to examine the implementation of the program standards that guide the school's character education program. The committee's purpose is to determine the extent to which the standards are being implemented. It is not our intention to repeat each of the standards listed in Chapter 2. The checklist below is an example of one way to assess the implementation of the standards.

Assessment Standards—A Checklist. In Chapter 2, we provided a list of program standards. As an example of how the CEEC might evaluate implementation of the standards, the following questions are suggested to help the committee understand our intent and construct their own questions for each of the standards.

☑ Have the various groups discussed why a character education program is important to the community at this time?

☑ Has discussion led to a clear and concise mission statement?

☑ Are goals and expectations stated in such a way that they help inform participants about processes, content, and evaluation?

☑ How well do the participants know the vision, goals, and expectations of the character education program?

☑ To what extent has the leadership educated the public about the need for and importance of the character education program?

☑ Has the leadership developed a plan to help the community reach consensus about which values should be fostered?

☑ To what extent has the public been invited to participate in helping promote the character education program?

☑ To what extent are community leaders and community organizations included in the character education efforts?

☑ What agencies and organizations need to be encouraged to take a more active role?

☑ How will individuals and groups who lack a power base be invited to contribute to the community's or school's character education efforts?

☑ What role has been created for children and youth in the character education program plans?

☑ Does a culture of caring permeate character education efforts?

☑ How is care demonstrated, practiced, and promoted by all participants?

☑ Are the criteria (the "11 C's") used as reference points for individuals and groups as they carry out their roles and responsibilities?

☑ Have adequate resources been allocated to implement the character education program?

☑ Are resources allocated for each of the standards (i.e., training, etc.)?

☑ Are there sufficient personnel for program implementation?

☑ Have parents been involved in the creation and implementation of the character education program?

☑ Are there specific activities that will help parents foster the consensus values in their homes?

☑ Has the community placed the schools and its educators in a leadership role for its character education programs?

☑ Have school personnel identified who will be the administrators of record for implementing and monitoring the school or school district's character education program?

☑ Have school personnel examined ways to involve the community and parents in school programs and activities?

☑ Have school personnel involved the community in obtaining funding and other resources to adequately conduct the character education program?

☑ Before program implementation, have all school personnel engaged in staff development programs and training?

☑ Have stakeholders been involved in discussions about the evaluation processes and procedures?

☑ Is there a program assessment plan that can be reviewed by parents and community groups?

☑ How effective is the community and school district in supporting each school's efforts to implement a character education program?

☑ How are new school personnel introduced to character education programs in the district or at the school site?

☑ How do the school culture and the classroom climate foster the criteria (the 11 C's) and the consensus values of the character education program?

☑ In what ways has the character education program strengthened the relationships among home, school, and community and between teachers and parents?

When the CEEC attends to these questions to be sure that the standards are being met, it will find the answers to be useful, informative, and guiding.

Task 6

Once the committee has adequately met the requirements implied in Task 5, it should determine how to evaluate and how best to prepare all participants for their roles in the process. Examples of informal instruments that may be used are presented later in this chapter.

Task 7

The evaluation committee should determine how it will handle the data resulting from the evaluation. Who will collect it? Who will analyze it? Who will summarize it?

Task 8

The evaluation committee must decide how best to report the findings and how to disseminate them to the participants and the community.

Task 9

The evaluation committee should refer to its timeline and determine its next steps.

TEN STEPS TO
SUCCESSFUL EVALUATION

Given the above tasks for the CEEC, we offer 10 steps for successful character education evaluation efforts.

Step 1: Organize for Assessment!

As we outlined in Chapter 2, there may be one of three patterns used for organizing character education programs for the community, school district, or school site. No matter which pattern is used, assessment matters must receive the same attention as do programmatic efforts. In fact, they should go hand in hand. It is clear from the recommendations above that as participants plan the character education program, they should also organize and plan the evaluation portion of the program.

The principle: Assessment strategies must accompany implementations plans.

Step 2: Know the Research/Read the Literature!

Stakeholders, and particularly educators, should know the literature on character education. They should read definitive texts, seminal articles, relevant research, and popular press pieces to get a sense of what this important topic is all about. Knowledge is power—the ability to answer questions, to know the issues, to engage in discussions and debate, and to inform and instruct. These are the basics for those who will take leadership roles in promoting character education in the schools and community. The research, the readings, and the resources at the end of the chapters in this book would be a good start.

The principle: Although a little knowledge is a dangerous thing, no knowledge could destroy the program.

Step 3: Asking the Right Questions!

Throughout this chapter, we use questions as a way to guide you through the standards, program implementation, and methods. Questions about assessment and, of course, the all-important answers help provide operational guidelines. The committee should address such questions as: What should be evaluated? Why should it be evaluated? Who should do the evaluation? When should it be evaluated? Where should it be evaluated? How should it be evaluated? What is an appropriate evaluation timetable? What resources will the committee need to get its work done?

The principle: If you don't ask the right questions, you may operate on the wrong premises.

Step 4: Evaluation—The Play's the Thing!

Everyone should be in the "evaluation play," from students to senior citizens, from teachers to custodians, from parents to politicians. Why? Because all will have opinions about the consensus values and the various programs. Furthermore, involvement in the evaluation process is educative. All will want to know: Are the programs working? What should be changed? What more needs to be done? Why should instructional time be taken up with character education when kids need to be taught the basics?

Other than quantifiable data coming from records and reports, qualitative evaluative methods, such as surveys, anecdotes, stories, narratives, observations, perceptions, self-reporting, questionnaires, checklists, and attitude instruments will provide useful information. All these need to tap a wide range of players in the community and in the school's or district's character education efforts.

The principle: The more people are involved in evaluative efforts, the more they will learn about the program and the greater the likelihood for support.

Step 5: Action Research Is Fun and Valuable!

Assessment means trying things out. It means creating your own action research projects. It means leaving the big things (correlational studies, experimental studies, comparative studies) to trained researchers. We recommend that local educators and community groups cooperatively create their own research plans; try out homemade evaluation instruments; learn to ask the right questions and figure out how best to answer them. They should test their own ways of trying to foster the values, use authentic assessment methods, create strategies that will involve others (particularly students and parents) in the research, and design unique and creative ways of reporting findings. The CEEC should develop a resource bank of questionnaires, rating scales, and other evaluative instruments that might be useful to school personnel for constructing their own informal instruments or to locate instruments that might serve their exact purposes.

For example, in his book *Positive Classroom Management* Robert DiGiulio (1995) has created a comprehensive prosocial classroom checklist of questions in the following areas: general, physical, instructional, and managerial. One item from each will illustrate the value to teachers (pp. 97-100).

General: Is it clear that respect is not negotiable?

Physical: Does my classroom feel like a safe and pleasant place to be?

Instructional: As I teach, do I communicate instructional expectations?

Managerial: When faced with misbehavior, do I maintain dignity—mine and the student's?

Another example of the development and use of informal instruments can be found in a book published by the National Middle School Association (Schurr, 1992). The book focuses on informal program evaluation strategies and includes samples of evaluation instruments, information to practitioners on how to customize evaluation plans, the use of technology in evaluation, evaluation tools and techniques, writing evaluation reports, and using evaluation results.

The principle: You don't have to be a trained researcher to do research, you just have to educate yourself and your group, be creative, and try things out.

Step 6: Get Help! Involve the Experts!

Our advice to the committee is not to try to do sophisticated assessment without help from the experts. There are plenty of evaluation specialists located in your community's businesses, community colleges, colleges and universities, district offices, state departments of education, and county offices of education. These experts should be brought in early in the planning process. They should serve as designers of the research that needs to accompany the character education implementation plans. They should provide ongoing advice and counsel and assist in data collection, analysis, and reporting.

The principle: When you need a specialist, going to a general practitioner may not help.

Step 7: Create an Assessment Cycle!

Fostering values takes time. Behavior changes in the young may not occur after a 6-week unit on "justice" or a year of community activities on learning and practicing "respect." There are no quick fixes for character education programs. The influence of school programs may not be revealed until students have left the school setting. Behavior, maturity, and life experiences may be influenced by the personal values and civic competencies taught at home, in the schools, and in the community. But we usually don't include evaluation strategies that attempt to trace these possible relationships. Like many others in society, the stakeholders may look for immediate payoffs. There may be few immediate or short-term outcomes from character education programs, but that should not prevent your stakeholders from exploring ways to get information about program effects and influences on students, school personnel, school and classroom climate, and community programs and activities.

Stakeholders and leaders involved in fostering the community's consensus values and its character education programs need time to get things started. For these reasons, a 4-year accountability cycle is recommended. Evaluation efforts should be ongoing, as we have suggested. But the CEEC will want to implement an accountability scheme, a community snapshot of where it is, what it is doing, what has been learned, and what has been accomplished at least every 4th year. In each school, that means assessment will take place in the 4th, 8th, and 12th grades. It means that educators will have to decide what is to be evaluated and when. Summative evaluation every 4th year is not intended to replace formative, ongoing assessment efforts during the program.

The principle: Plan for long-term assessment but take
                  "pictures" along the way.

Step 8: Communication!

One side of the "what" question is what programs and activities will be created and implemented to promote the community's, the school district's, or the school site's character education program goals and objectives? The other side of that question is what influence do the character education programs have on children and youth? The committee should report information, on a regular basis, about what it is doing, why it is doing it, how effective it thinks the programs are (evidence would help here), and of what worth these programs are to the school and community. Such reporting ensures the "communication" portion of the framework, encourages discussion, promotes cooperative efforts, dispels rumors, and corrects misperceptions.

The principle: Effective communication forms connections and leads to collaboration.

Step 9: Designs

We recommend a mix of assessment methods, but we strongly suggest that the committee let its evaluation experts help guide the designs that best fit with the expectations of the program and what and how such expectations are to be evaluated. Some researchers like comparative, controlled studies because of the useful information such studies provide when comparing groups of students who have been exposed to a "treatment" (the character education program) and those who have not. Others prefer what is called "ethnographic," or qualitative research (surveys, teacher and student testimony, etc.), providing in-depth observations and rich descriptions of what is going on in the schools.

The principle: Create research designs that serve both your summative and formative evaluation needs.

Step 10: Cautions

Evaluation plans that would cause public debate should be avoided so as not to detract from the main purposes of the character education program. Be careful about the interpretation of the results of any evaluation. Be aware that not all positive findings suggest simple cause-and-effect relationships. Try to include quantitative data to support qualitative analysis and vice versa.

The principle. Don't jump to unwarranted, insupportable conclusions.

EVALUATION: NINE EXAMPLES

In the next section, we provide examples of ways to evaluate (or at least collect data about) certain aspects of a character education program. These examples are illustrative and should be modified by the CEEC to meet local needs and expectations.

Example 1: A Character Education Evaluation Effectiveness Scale

The Character Education Partnership (Lickona, Schaps, & Lewis, 1996) published a list of 11 principles of effective character education. Lickona designed a formative assessment instrument called the "Eleven Principles Survey (EPS) of Character Education Effectiveness," addressing the question: To what extent is the school implementing these eleven principles? The author states that the survey may be a self-assessment instrument or it may be used by an outside observer. The scale yields three scores: one score for each subcomponent of each principle, one score for each principle, and an overall score.[1]

Eleven Principles Survey (EPS) of Character Education Effectiveness

Directions to the Individual Completing the Survey:

1. *On the basis of your own observations, rate the degree to which you think the following character education principles are implemented in your school.* Please give your honest opinions, since candid responses provide the most valid data. If

you do not have enough knowledge of a particular item to give it a rating, circle "Don't know" (DK).

2. *Please record your ratings on the individual EPS response form, as well as on the survey itself.* Then submit the individual EPS response form to the person summarizing the data for your school. *Keep* your copy of the survey, with your rating, to use in staff discussion of the schoolwide survey results.

3. *Indicate your school position* (administrator, teacher, professional support staff, classified staff, parent, etc.) on the individual form *but not your name.* Responses are meant to be anonymous.

The rating scale following each principle's subcomponents is

Low Implementation			High Implementation		
1____	2____	3____	4____	5____	DK
					(Don't know)

1. CHARACTER EDUCATION PROMOTES AND TEACHES QUALITIES OF GOOD CHARACTER, OR VIRTUES, SUCH AS *PRUDENCE (GOOD JUDGMENT), RESPECT, RESPONSIBILITY, HONESTY, FAIRNESS, COURTESY, KINDNESS, COURAGE, DILIGENCE, PERSEVERANCE, AND SELF-CONTROL.*

   1.1 Our school staff and parent community have agreed on the character traits we wish to promote in our character education program.

   1.2 We have defined these character traits in terms of behaviors that can be observed in the school, family, and community.

   1.3 We have made these character traits and their behavioral definitions widely known throughout our school and parent community.

2. CHARACTER IS DEFINED COMPREHENSIVELY TO INCLUDE THINKING, FEELING, AND BEHAVIOR.

   2.1 We take deliberate steps to help students acquire a developmentally appropriate understanding of what the character traits mean in everyday behavior and to grasp the reasons why some behaviors are right and others are wrong.

2.2 We take deliberate steps to help students admire the character traits, desire to possess them, and become committed to them.

2.3 We take deliberate steps to help students practice the character traits so that they become habits.

3. CHARACTER EDUCATION IS INTENTIONAL, PROACTIVE, AND COMPREHENSIVE.

3.1 Our program is intentional and proactive; it provides regular, planned, and explicit opportunities for students to learn the qualities of good character.

3.2 Our program is comprehensive across the curriculum; the character traits are regularly integrated into instruction in all subjects and at all grade levels.

3.3 Our character program is infused throughout the school days. The character traits are upheld by adults, and are taken seriously by students throughout the school environment: in classrooms, corridors, cafeterias, assemblies, and extracurricular activities, and on playgrounds, athletic fields, and school buses.

3.4 Our drug, alcohol, and sex education programs are character-based, consistent with the school's highest character expectations of respect, responsibility, and self-control, and actively guide students toward abstinence from drugs, alcohol, and sexual activity.

4. THE SCHOOL IS A CARING COMMUNITY.

4.1 Our school makes it a high priority to foster caring attachments among adults and students. The school schedule, for example, is designed to minimize disruption and stress and to maximize staff time for developing supportive relationships with their students.

4.2 Our school makes it a high priority to help students form caring attachments to each other, including caring attachments between older and younger students.

4.3 Our school does not tolerate peer cruelty (persecution, exclusion, and the like) and takes steps to prevent and deal with it effectively when it occurs.

5. STUDENTS HAVE FREQUENT OPPORTUNITIES FOR MORAL ACTION.

5.1 Our program provides students with repeated and varied opportunities for moral action such as cooperative learning, conflict resolution, class problem-solving meetings, classroom helper jobs, peer tutoring, school and community service, and taking personal responsibility for improving one's behavior or learning.

5.2 Our program helps students consciously take responsibility for developing their own character—for example, by encouraging students to set daily goals to practice the character traits and to assess and record their success in achieving their goals.

6. CHARACTER EDUCATION INCLUDES AN ACADEMIC CURRICULUM THAT BUILDS GOOD CHARACTER.

6.1 Our academic curriculum is designed to challenge all students to do their personal best and to develop the qualities of character, such as self-discipline, diligence, perseverance, and a concern for excellence, that support personal responsibility and a strong work ethic.

6.2 Our school respects the way students learn by providing active learning experiences such as problem solving, cooperative learning, and projects that build on students' interests.

6.3 Our curriculum recognizes multiple intelligences and helps students of diverse abilities and needs to discover and develop their special talents.

7. CHARACTER EDUCATION STRIVES TO DEVELOP THE INTRINSIC MOTIVATION CENTRAL TO GOOD CHARACTER.

7.1 Our program's approach to classroom and school discipline is centered on developing students' intrinsic commitment to doing what's right—following legitimate rules, for example, because doing so respects the rights and needs of self and others. Logical consequences for wrongdoing are administered in such a way as to strengthen a student's inner character resources, including moral reasoning, self-control, and strategies for responsible behavior in the future. Students are also taught to take initiative to make active restitution when they do something wrong.

7.2 When we deal with discipline problems, we make explicit reference to the character qualities we are trying to teach—with the goal of helping students use standards such as courtesy, kindness, honesty, fairness, and self-control to evaluate and improve their conduct.

7.3 In our classrooms and school, we recognize and celebrate good character in ways that support rather than undermine intrinsic motivation (by keeping the focus on doing good things because it helps others and oneself). Recognition for good character is accessible to all who are deserving and not limited to just a few.

8. THE ENTIRE SCHOOL STAFF SHARES RESPONSIBILITY FOR CHARACTER EDUCATION AND LIVES BY THE SCHOOL'S CHARACTER EXPECTATIONS.

8.1 All professional school staff (including administrators, counselors, librarians, and teaching faculty) have been included in planning, receiving staff development for, and carrying out the schoolwide character education effort.

8.2 All nonprofessional staff (including secretaries, cafeteria workers, bus drivers, playground aides, etc.) have been included in planning, receiving staff development for, and carrying out the school-wide character education effort.

8.3 The character traits espoused by our school are modeled by staff in their interactions with students.

8.4 The character traits espoused by our school are practiced by staff in their interactions with each other; there is a moral community among adults, including relations between administration and faculty, that is governed by norms of mutual respect, fairness, and collaborative decision making.

8.5 Regular and adequate time is made available for staff planning and reflection: to design the character education program, share success stories, assess progress, and address moral concerns, especially gaps between the school's professed character expectations and observed behavior in the school.

9. CHARACTER EDUCATION INVOLVES MORAL LEADERSHIP BY STAFF AND STUDENTS.

9.1 Our program has a leader (the principal, another administrator, a lead teacher) who champions our character education effort.

9.2 There is a leadership group (a committee, a task force) that guides the ongoing planning and implementation of our character education program and encourages the involvement of the whole school.

9.3 Students are involved in leadership roles (e.g., through student government, special councils, and peer mediation) in ways that develop their responsibility and help the school's character expectations become part of the peer culture.

10. THE SCHOOL RECRUITS PARENTS AND THE COMMUNITY AS FULL PARTNERS IN CHARACTER EDUCATION.

10.1 Our program explicitly affirms that parents are the first and most important moral educators of their children. Parents' questions and concerns about any part of our character education program are taken seriously. Every effort is made to respect parents' rights as their child's primary moral educator.

10.2 Our program asks parents to identify the character qualities that should be fostered by the school.

10.3 Parents are included in our school's character education leadership group.

10.4 All parents are informed about the goals and teaching methods of our character education program.

10.5 Our school sends home communications (such as letters from the principal) and suggestions (such as dinner discussion topics and bedtime reading) that help parents reinforce the character qualities the school is trying to teach. Our school also offers workshops, parenting tips, books, tapes, and other resources that help parents develop their general parenting skills and strengthen their relationship with their child.

10.6 Our school has involved representatives of the wider community (e.g., businesses, religious institutions, youth organizations, government, and the media) in helping to plan our character education effort.

10.7 Our school involves the wider community as partners in character education, including community-based efforts to promote the qualities of good character.

11. CHARACTER EDUCATION ASSESSES THE CHARACTER OF THE SCHOOL, THE SCHOOL STAFF'S FUNCTIONING AS CHARACTER EDUCATORS, AND THE CHARACTER DEVELOPMENT OF STUDENTS.

11.1 Our program assesses the character of our school as a moral community (e.g., through school climate surveys using agree/disagree items such as, "Students in our school respect each other" and "Our school is like a family.")

11.2 Our staff periodically engages in systematic assessment of our program, using surveys such as this to determine the degree to which we are implementing the intended components of our character education program. The results of these assessments are used to plan program improvements.

11.3 Our school asks staff to report (through questionnaires, anecdotal records) their efforts periodically to implement character education.

11.4 We assess our students' progress in developing an understanding of the character traits—for example, by asking them to define the traits, recognize or produce examples of the traits in action, and explain how these traits help them and others.

11.5 We assess our students' progress in developing an emotional attachment and commitment to the qualities of good character—for example, by asking students to rate how important the character traits are to them in their lives.

11.6 We assess our students' progress in behaving in ways that reflect the character traits—for example, by collecting data on observable character-related behaviors such as school attendance, acts of honesty, volunteering for school or community service, discipline referrals, fighting, vandalism, drug incidents, student pregnancies, and by asking students to complete anonymous self-report questionnaires on character-related behaviors (e.g., "How may times during the past week have you helped someone who is not a friend or a family member?" "How many times in the past month have you stood up for what is right—for example, by resisting peer pressure to do something wrong or by defending a schoolmate against unfair gossip?" and "How may times have you cheated on a test or major assignment in the past year?").

11.7 We include assessment of student character as part of our report card.

The survey can be summarized using the average of the individual ratings for each principle. The scales for Principles 1 and 2 are shown below as examples.

1. Overall rating for Principle 1: _____ *(average of ratings of the subcomponents)*

          Rating for Subcomponent 1.1 _____
          Rating for Subcomponent 1.2 _____
          Rating for Subcomponent 1.3 _____

2. Overall rating for Principle 2: _____

          Rating for Subcomponent 2.1 _____
          Rating for Subcomponent 2.2 _____
          Rating for Subcomponent 2.3 _____

Example 2: School Personnel's Perceptions of the
Character Education Program

The CEEC decides that, near the end of the first year or later, it wishes to find out how school personnel view their character education program. The CEEC creates an informal perception scale on which the respondent chooses one response for each item, such as no opinion, definitely, sometimes, or not at all. Suggested items include the following:

_____ 1. There is a rationale for the school's character education program.

_____ 2. Most people at this school know the consensus values and expectations of the character education program.

_____ 3. I have been (or I was) adequately prepared to begin the program.

_____ 4. Parents have been a significant part of the planning and implementation of the program.

_____ 5. School leaders have involved the community in supporting our efforts.

_____ 6. Teachers have examined the curriculum to determine how best to integrate the consensus values into each subject.

_____ 7. We have developed school-wide plans and activities for fostering the consensus values.

_____ 8. The school administration has been very supportive of efforts to implement the character education program.

_____ 9. Our plans and procedures have brought teachers and others together in collaborative efforts.

_____ 10. The program has improved students' social behaviors.

_____ 11. The school's supporting services (guidance, health, etc.) are helping teachers and students meet the expectations of the program.

_____ 12. Students report that they notice more positive behaviors now than before the program started.

_____ 13. Most teachers report that the consensus values being fostered in the school have had a positive effect on the climate of their classrooms.

_____ 14. Visitors to the school report a positive school environment.

_____ 15. The character education program has contributed to enhancing the academic program.

Example 3: School's Problems Inventory

Suppose the committee decides that it wants to collect baseline data before the character education program is implemented and compare it with the data collected 3 years into the program. In other words, the committee is interested in determining the extent to which the character education program may have caused positive changes in all or some of the items in the inventory. To find out, it uses an inventory similar to the one suggested below.

In the school's problems inventory, the "N" represents the actual number of students and the "%" represents the percentage of the students in the school. The "N" and the "%" are listed only for the first three items as an example. "BPI" means "Before Program Implementation."

Of course, baseline data might also be collected, examined, and communicated that stresses the positive student behaviors as well as the negative student behaviors. For example, on the positive side, information could be gathered about the number and percentages of students who receive high grades, honors, and recognitions; participate in school activities; assume leadership roles; participate in academic contests and fairs; and volunteer at the school and in the com-

---

School Problems Inventory for _____ *School*

BPI	ITEM	YEAR THREE
N____%____	A. Student truancy	N____%____
N____%____	B. Student dropouts	N____%____
N____%____	C. Student absentees	N____%____
	D. Office referrals	
	E. Recorded problems	
	F. Incidences of cheating	
	G. Vandalism—school property	
	H. Vandalism—student property	
	I. Student expulsions	
	J. Student suspensions	
	K. Physical abuse of students	
	L. Racial/ethnic incidences	
	M. Sexual harassment	
	N. Thefts—school property	
	O. Thefts—student property	
	P. Thefts—school personnel property	
	Q. Other (_____)	

---

munity. Students who work part-time and maintain good grades, and who participate in some school and community activities should not be overlooked.

Example 4: Students' Misbehaviors and
Probable Causes

The Character Education Evaluation Committee (CEEC) wishes to find out from school personnel (and maybe from students themselves) about the frequency of certain student misbehaviors and the probable causes of such behaviors. (See Figure 6.1.)

Figure 6.1. Students' Misbehaviors/Offenses Inventory

Directions: This inventory attempts to find out how you feel about the frequency of student misbehaviors / offenses in this school (class, group) and the probable causes. Place a check mark on one of the lines under *Frequency* (excessive, moderate, or rare) and circle those numbers that reflect your view of the causes for the misbehavior/offense using the following guide:

1—home environment
2—parent attitude
3—lack of parental control
4—peer group influence

5—school or teacher caused
6—students have personal problems
7—students have learning problems
8—all of the causes

	Frequency			Causes
Offenses	*Excessive*	*Moderate*	*Rare*	
1. Habitual tardiness	——	——	——	1 2 3 4 5 6 7 8
2. Regularly skipping class	——	——	——	1 2 3 4 5 6 7 8
3. Truancy, poor attendance	——	——	——	1 2 3 4 5 6 7 8
4. Cheating	——	——	——	1 2 3 4 5 6 7 8
5. Disruptive behavior	——	——	——	1 2 3 4 5 6 7 8
6. Continual inattention in class	——	——	——	1 2 3 4 5 6 7 8
7. Rowdiness	——	——	——	1 2 3 4 5 6 7 8
8. Persistent silent contempt	——	——	——	1 2 3 4 5 6 7 8

(continued)

Figure 6.1. Continued

Offenses	Frequency			Causes
	Excessive	Moderate	Rare	
9. Sneering, muttering	___	___	___	1 2 3 4 5 6 7 8
10. Swearing	___	___	___	1 2 3 4 5 6 7 8
11. Carries weapons	___	___	___	1 2 3 4 5 6 7 8
12. Unacceptable sexual behavior	___	___	___	1 2 3 4 5 6 7 8
13. Physical assaults on students	___	___	___	1 2 3 4 5 6 7 8
14. Physical assaults on teachers, other adults	___	___	___	1 2 3 4 5 6 7 8
15. Excessive talking	___	___	___	1 2 3 4 5 6 7 8
16. Lack of interest	___	___	___	1 2 3 4 5 6 7 8
17. Not listening	___	___	___	1 2 3 4 5 6 7 8
18. Destructive of school property	___	___	___	1 2 3 4 5 6 7 8
19. Destructive of student property	___	___	___	1 2 3 4 5 6 7 8
20. Drug/alcohol use	___	___	___	1 2 3 4 5 6 7 8
21. Disrespect, not courteous	___	___	___	1 2 3 4 5 6 7 8
22. Failure to complete school work	___	___	___	1 2 3 4 5 6 7 8
23. Smoking	___	___	___	1 2 3 4 5 6 7 8
24. Other (list)	___	___	___	1 2 3 4 5 6 7 8

Example 5: Community Involvement Inventory

In this example, the CEEC's intention is to help the school's Character Education Council gather information about the extent to which businesses and organizations are involved or want to be involved in the community's or school's character education programs. The intent is to find a "niche" in the programs for various groups, companies, and organizations. The following form might be sent to local companies, the media, the chamber of commerce, churches, parent groups, civic groups, law enforcement agencies, youth service agencies, and the like. Or the statements on the form may be used for telephone interviews of a sample of the possible respondents.

Company _____

Address _____

Name of Respondent _____

1. During the past year, did your company participate in any of the school's/community's character education programs?
   YES _____   NO _____

2. If NO, please state the reason(s):

3. If YES, place a "Y" next to the item(s) in which your company has participated. If NO, place an "I" next to any item that your company may be interested in as part of its contribution to the school's/community's character education efforts.

   _____ Student field trips to the company

   _____ Financial support for school/community project

   _____ Special holiday events

   _____ Student recognition activities

   _____ PTA program/activities

   _____ Guest speakers at school assemblies/in classes

____ Sponsor specific activities at the request of the school

____ Speakers on character education at company meetings

____ Allow employees time off for school activities/programs

____ Provide scholarships

____ Support youth groups/activities

____ Display character education posters/student work

____ Support community character education activities

____ Sponsor student leadership groups/activities

____ Place character education information in publications

____ Underwrite the cost of character education materials

____ Employees serve on boards, councils, committees

____ Tutoring or mentoring activities

____ Self-esteem activities

____ School campus and in-school beautification needs

____ Parent outreach activities

____ Assist with student council, clubs, Junior Achievement

____ Assist with staff development needs

____ Share expertise in team building, group decision making

____ Other (please specify)

4. What information, if any, does your company need to take a more active role in this community's character education efforts?

5. What factors prevent your company from taking an active role in the school's/community's character education efforts?

6. How would you rate your company leaders' knowledge of the school's / community's character education goals and programs?

7. Are you willing to be contacted by a member of the Character Education Council to discuss goals and programs?
YES____ NO____

If yes, please provide your phone number and the best time to call:_____

Example 6: Assessing Student Views—A Questionnaire

Suppose the CEEC decides to poll students (middle and upper grades) after the first year of the character education program to determine their views about the effectiveness and influence of the program on them and their peers. To do this, CEEC constructs a questionnaire using sample questions and items, such as the ones listed below, and asks participants to grade each (when appropriate) on a scale from A to F.

_____ Since the character education program was implemented in this school, have you noticed any positive changes? If yes, describe these changes. If no, tell us why.

_____ What grade would you give your friends at school for the way they practice or show that they have learned most of the values?

_____ In what ways did *you* show that one or more of the values was important to you?

_____ Grade the extent to which you feel the values are part of the subjects you study at this school.

_____ Grade the extent to which you feel the values are part of the entire school environment.

_____ Would you agree or disagree with this statement: "For the most part, this school has become a more caring place since the character education program started." Why?

_____ What would make the school's character education program more meaningful to you and other students?

_____ What grade would you give to this school's character education program?

Example 7: Student Portfolios

As educators know, student portfolios are collections of artifacts and reflections that document a student's work over time. This next

suggestion is a variation on that idea. As a result of an inservice program on assessment, the CEEC asks teachers to try out this version
of portfolio assessment or to infuse the consensus values into the
content of the portfolios that they may be currently using. Each
teacher is asked to organize students into teams (two members) or
small groups (three to five members). Each team/group develops a
portfolio that focuses on one of the values in the character education
program. For example, one team may take the value of "honesty,"
another group may select "respect," and another may pick "self-discipline." Over time, their task is to create a portfolio on that value.
The portfolio may include such items as the following:

- A summary of writings about the value
- A team journal recording observations and feelings about the value
- Drawings, cartoons, and comics with a description of how the authors illustrate the value
- Book reviews that describe how the stories depict the value
- Collection of poems, stories, or tales about the value
- Clippings from newspapers and magazines that relate to the value
- Reviews of television programs that promote or defame the value
- Reviews of how the value is promoted or defamed by political and business leaders, professional athletes, and celebrities
- Recommendations for helping other students learn about the value
- Posters of quotes, sayings, axioms
- Reflection on character education efforts in the school
- Descriptive answers to reflective questions, such as the following:

    What influence has this assignment/this portfolio had on your (team/group) knowledge and practice of this value?

    What did you learn about this value that you didn't know before you created this portfolio?

What should be done with the contents of your portfolio? How do you think it should be graded?

Are you willing to share your portfolio with others?

What ways would you suggest that the teams/groups in this classroom share their portfolios?

Describe incidents where the value that you have selected has been demonstrated in real-life situations.

Describe observations where the value was applied in your school, in your neighborhood, and by your friends.

Example 8: Polling Parents

There are many ways to determine parent knowledge and assess their views, perceptions, and involvement in the school's character education program (see Chapter 5). An example of an "opinionnaire" that might be administered sometime after the school's character education program is under way is shown below. Only 10 items are listed in the example. The list should include the consensus values being fostered and promoted at the school. Opinionnaires such as this one can also be designed for teachers, students, and other school personnel. The opinionnaire should be published in the primary language of the parents.

Parent Opinionnaire

Directions to Parents: The_____[name of school] Character Education Evaluation Committee is interested in your opinion regarding efforts to foster the values of [list the consensus values of the program here] and the influences these values may have on the behaviors of students. We ask that you take a few minutes to complete this opinionnaire. Your name is not necessary. Please return it within 5 days using the enclosed self-addressed stamped envelope.

In your opinion, what *positive effect* has the character education program had on your son/daughter with regard to the following items (check one for each numbered item):

	Great	Moderate	Little	None
1. Caring about others	____	____	____	____
2. Attitude toward school	____	____	____	____
3. Attitude toward teachers	____	____	____	____
4. Self-discipline	____	____	____	____
5. Responsibility	____	____	____	____
6. Attitude toward adults	____	____	____	____
7. Emotional skills	____	____	____	____
8. Attitude toward school work	____	____	____	____
9. Tolerance of others	____	____	____	____
10. Social skills	____	____	____	____

Now tell us what *positive effect* the character education program has had on the *STUDENTS* in your son's/daughter's classes or their friends with regard to each of the following items:

	Great	Moderate	Little	None
1. Caring about others	____	____	____	____
2. Attitude toward school	____	____	____	____
3. Attitude toward teachers	____	____	____	____
4. Self-discipline	____	____	____	____
5. Responsibility	____	____	____	____
6. Attitude toward adults	____	____	____	____
7. Emotional skills	____	____	____	____
8. Attitude toward school work	____	____	____	____
9. Tolerance of others	____	____	____	____
10. Social skills	____	____	____	____

The 10 items on the scale are merely examples. You could substitute specific character traits such as honesty, courtesy, respect, compassion, caring, civility, courage, loyalty, fairness, and so on.

Example 9: Classroom Climate

There are many ways and a variety of instruments to assess the extent to which the classroom environment supports the tenets of the school's character education program.

For example, Vessels (1998, pp. 230-240) provides two survey instruments, one for early elementary grades and the other for later elementary grades. Both have been field-tested in the Atlanta Public Schools.

In another example, Schaps (1999, p. 31), who has written extensively about the Child Development Project, provides an instrument that measures the classroom as a learning community.

To these and other resources, we add our own instrument that might best be used in grades 5–12. A teacher who uses this classroom-climate opinionnaire would be seeking the students' views about relationships and responsibilities.

Your Views—Your Voice

Directions: I want to hear from you about relationships and responsibilities in our class. There are no right or wrong answers. I want and need your opinions. So take the next 15 minutes to think about your answers to each question and write them down, but do not sign your name. I will collect them when you have finished.

A. List five things you like about this class:

1. _____

2. _____

3. _____

4. _____

5. _____

B. List five things that bother you about this class:

   1. _____

   2. _____

   3. _____

   4. _____

   5. _____

C. Tell me your views about the way I teach:

   I like _____

   I don't like _____

D. Tell me your views about your classmates:

   I like _____

   I don't like _____

E. Tell me three things that you like best about our classroom:

   1. _____

   2. _____

   3. _____

F. Tell me three things that you like least about our classroom:

   1. _____

   2. _____

   3. _____

G. How do you feel about your relationship with me?

H. How do you feel about your relationship with your classmates?

I. If you were the teacher in this classroom, what would you do to make it a better place to teach and learn?

An Evaluation Plan in Practice

We report here an example of how a character education program in the St. Louis area, Character Plus (formerly PREP), is organized to evaluate programs that, in 1996, reached 22 public school districts, 275 schools, and 185,000 students (Network for Educational Development, 1994).

First, an external evaluation consultant works with the Character Plus Development Team to plan annual and long-term program evaluation plans.

Second, the program evaluation plan focuses on three major questions:

1. Was the program implemented as designed?

2. Were the student outcomes met?

3. Is the program being institutionalized and disseminated in the district?

Third, data collection includes quantitative evidence (e.g., number of schools and students involved, spread of program, number of educator preparation programs, etc.), student data (e.g., changes in truancy, reports to the office, dropout rates, etc.), and qualitative evidence (e.g., reports from participants, reports from observers, interviews, material reviews, etc.). The booklet in which this evaluation plan is described also includes a sample survey instrument for students and for teachers and administrators (Network for Educational Development, 1994, pp. 34-35).

Fourth, the external evaluator conducts an annual survey of Character Plus teachers and students.

Fifth, outside experts make site visits and report results to the external evaluator.

Sixth, at the end of each school year, each district submits a report to the external evaluator who critiques it.

Seventh, each year's evaluation report includes an introduction, program description, evaluation questions, methods, findings, conclusions and implications, and recommendations (also see Character Plus at the end of Chapter 2).

A CONCLUDING WORD

We have suggested that each school district and each school site create an evaluation committee. Guidelines, principles, questions, and methods were presented as examples and idea-generators for individuals and committees who not only want to but should evaluate their character education efforts. As more and more schools implement character education programs and as the public continues to support character development efforts, will we as educators take the time to better train ourselves to do the job? Will we enhance our evaluative skills and interests? Will we attempt to decide whether or not what we teach really works? Will we try to find out whether or not what we practice really works? Will we try to find out whether the character education program that our schools have planned will influence student behavior in some positive way? Will we encourage others to find out if the program changes the "ethos" of the school and the climate of the classroom? Will we ask whether the program changed relationships among the stakeholders?

The answers will be forthcoming because the public is calling for more accountability with regard to the schools' academic programs and its affect on student achievement (translate—test scores). They will, in time, ask for character education program results as well. Stakeholders and leaders should be prepared for the public's request for accountability.

QUOTES:
Something to Think About

It is no coincidence that the word VALUE is embedded in evaluation. If evaluation is the process of comparing something to a standard or value, then self-evaluation engages students in that task, requiring them to compare themselves and their work to some criteria or standard of value.

—*Kirschenbaum, H. (1995). 100 ways to enhance values and morality in school and youth settings. Boston: Allyn & Bacon, p. 190.*

We humans are remarkably prone to form partisan distinctions between our own and other groups, to develop a marked preference for our group, to accept favorable evaluations of the product and performances of the in-group, and to make unfavorable evaluations of groups that go far beyond the objective evidence or the requirements of a situation.

—Hamburg, D. H. (1994).
Education for conflict resolution.
New York: Carnegie Corporation of New York, p. 6.

Schools are settings that mediate the diversity of a pluralistic society. Schools indeed have been the classic center for bringing together people of different backgrounds; they have been the place that helps develop the skills of community, of learning to live with others who have different interests. Schools have been the classic American "place."

—Cohen, B., & Lukinsky, J. (1985).
Religious institutions as educators.
Eighty-Fourth Yearbook of the National Society
for the Study of Education.
University of Chicago Press, p. 153.

QUESTIONS:
Something to Talk About

1. If you have started a character education program and did not collect baseline data, how would you demonstrate that the program is meeting your and others' expectations?

2. What are the obstacles to assessing your school's/community's character education program?

3. What kinds of assistance would you, your school, and your community need to do an evaluation of the character education program?

4. What are the attitudes of people in your school about evaluating the extent to which they are successful in fostering the values of the character education program?

5. How would you apply some of the ideas in this chapter (e.g., standards, steps to success, examples) to the character education program in your school and community?

BOOKS:
Something to Read About

Heath, D. (1994). *Schools of hope: Developing minds and character in today's youth.* San Francisco: Jossey-Bass.

Huffman, H. A. (1994). *Developing a character education program: One school district's experience.* Alexandria, VA: Association for Supervision and Curriculum Development.

Vessels, G. (1998). *Character and community development: A school planning and teacher training handbook.* Westport, CT: Praeger.

Wynne, E. A., & Ryan, M. (1997). *Reclaiming our schools: A handbook on teaching character, academics, and discipline* (2nd ed.). New York: Macmillan.

PROGRAMS:
Something to Investigate

Resolving Conflict Creatively Program (RCCP)

Program: RCCP's intent is to show young people that there are many ways to deal with conflict besides passivity and aggression, to provide a range of skills to help them make real choices in their lives, to increase their understanding and appreciation of their own and other cultures, and to convince them that they can have a major role in creating a more peaceful world. This school-based program in conflict resolution and intergroup relations provides a model for preventing violence and for creating schools that are caring, learning communities. The program's primary strategy for reaching young people is professional development of the adults in their lives—principals, teachers, and parents.

Results: An independent evaluation (May 1990) found the following: the program had an effect on students, participating staff, and classroom climate that was both observable and quantifiable; teachers reported using conflict resolution lessons, as well as infusing the concepts into the curriculum; 98% of the teachers agreed that mediation gave children trained as mediators an important tool for dealing with everyday conflicts between students; 71% of the teachers surveyed said the program led to less physical violence in the classroom; teachers reported a decrease in verbal put-downs and an increase in students' initiative, leadership skills, and self-esteem; and teachers reported greater ability on their part to handle angry students and to deal with conflict in general (Lantieri, 1995).

Contact: Linda Lantieri, Director, RCCP National Center, 163 Third Avenue, #103, New York, NY 10003; Tel: (212) 387-0225.

NOTE

1. The Eleven Principles Survey is used with permission of Professor Thomas Lickona, Center for the 4th and 5th Rs, SUNY Cortland, P. O. Box 2000, NY 13045; (607) 753-2455. Further information about scoring sheets and process may be obtained at this address.

Resources

In this list of resources, we include Web sites for as many character-education organizations as possible. We know that Web site links, along with phone numbers or addresses, change over time. To ensure that the links are regularly updated and that you have access to a much wider range of organizations and programs online than can be listed here, we direct you to the Web site at the University of San Diego's International Center for Character Education: http://teachvalues.org.

CHARACTER EDUCATION ORGANIZATIONS

Center for the Advancement of Ethics and Character
Boston University
605 Commonwealth Avenue
Boston, MA 02215
(617) 353-3262 / (617) 353-3924 (fax)
http://education.bu.edu/characterEd

Center for Civic Education
5146 Douglas Fir Road
Calabasas, CA 91302-1467
(818) 591-9321 / (818) 591-9330 (fax)
http://www.civiced.org

The Center for Collaborative Education
An Affiliate of the Coalition of Essential Schools
1573 Madison Ave., Rm. 201
New York, NY 10029-3899
(212) 348-7821 / (212) 348-7850 (fax)
http://www.cce.org

Center for the Fourth and Fifth R's (Respect/Responsibility)
S.U.N.Y., Cortland, Education Department
P.O. Box 2000
Cortland, NY 13045
(607) 753-2455 / (607) 753-5980 (fax)
http://www.cortland.edu/www/c4n5rs

Character Development Group
P.O. Box 9211
Chapel Hill, NC 27515-9211
(919) 967-2110 / (919) 967-2139 (fax)
E-mail: respect96@aol.com
http://www.charactereducation.com

Character Education Institute
8918 Tesoro Drive, Suite 575
San Antonio, TX 78217-6253
(800) 284-0499 / (210) 829-1729 (fax)
http://www.charactereducation.org

Character Education Institute at California University
250 University Avenue
California, PA 15419-1394
(412) 938-4500 / (412) 938-4141 (fax)
http://www.cup.edu/character_ed

Character Plus [formerly PREP]
Cooperating School Districts
CEC 2000
8225 Florissant Rd.
St. Louis, MO 63121
(800) 478-5684 x4522 / (314) 516-4599 (fax)
http://info.csd.org/staffdev/chared/characterplus.html

Center for Youth Citizenship (CYC)
9738 Lincoln Village Drive
Sacramento, CA 95827
(916) 228-2322 / (916) 228-2493 (fax)
http://www.clre.org

Communitarian Network
2130 H Street, NW, Suite 703
Washington, DC 20052
(202) 994-7997
http://www.gwu.edu/~ccps

Community of Caring
1325 G Street, NW
Washington, DC 20005
(202) 393-1251 / (202) 824-0351 (fax)
http://www.communityofcaring.org

The Council for Global Education
P.O. Box 57218
Washington, DC 20036-9998
(202) 496-9780 / (202) 496 9781 (fax)
http://www.globaleducation.org

Developmental Studies Center
2000 Embarcadero, Suite 305
Oakland, CA 94606-5300
(510) 533-0213 / (510) 464-3670 (fax)
http://www.devstu.org

Educators for Social Responsibility
23 Garden Street
Cambridge, MA 02138
(800) 370-2515 / (617) 864-5164
http://www.esrnational.org

Ethics Resource Center
1747 Pennsylvania Avenue, NW, Suite 400
Washington, DC 20005
(202) 737-2258 / (202) 737-2227 (fax)
http://www.ethics.org

The Giraffe Project
P.O. Box 759, 197 Second Street
Langley, WA 98260
(360) 221-7989 / (360) 221-7817 (fax)
http://www.giraffe.org

Heartwood Institute
425 N. Craig Street, Suite 302
Pittsburgh, PA 15213
(412) 688-8570 / (412) 688-8552 (fax)
http.//www.enviroweb.org/heartwood

Institute for Global Ethics
11 Main Street, P.O. Box 563
Camden, ME 04843
(207) 236-6658 / (207) 236-4014 (fax)
http://www.globalethics.org

International Center for Character Education
University of San Diego
5998 Alcala Park
San Diego, CA 92110
(619) 260-5980 / (619) 260-7480 (fax)
http://teachvalues.org

International Educational Foundation
4 West 43rd Street
New York, NY 10036
(212) 944-7466 / (212) 944-6683 (fax)
http://www.iefcharactered.org

The Kenan Ethics Program, Duke University
Box 90432, 102 West Duke Building
Durham, NC 27708
(919) 660-3033 / (919) 660-3049 (fax)
http://kenan.ethics.duke.edu

Quest International
1984 Coffman Road, P.O. Box 4850
Newark, OH 43058-4850
(800) 446-2700 / (614) 522-6580 (fax)
http://www.quest.edu

School Development Program
Yale Child Study Center
55 College Street
New Haven, CT 06510
(203) 737-1020 / (203) 737-1023 (fax)
http://pandora.med.yale.edu/comer/quicklook.html

School for Ethical Education
440 Wheelers Farm Road
Milford, CT 06460
(203) 783-4439 / (203) 783-4464 (fax)
http://www.ethicsed.org

SERVICE LEARNING
ORGANIZATIONS

American Youth Foundation
2331 Hampton Avenue
St. Louis, MO 63104
(314) 646-6000 / (314) 772-7542 (fax)
http://www.ayf.com

Learn & Serve America
Corporation for National Service
1201 New York Avenue, NW
Washington, DC 20525
(202) 606-5000
http://www.cns.gov/learn/index.html

Learning for Life, Boy Scouts of America
1325 W. Walnut Hill Lane, P.O. Box 152079
Irving, TX 75015-2079
(972) 580-2000
http://www.learning-for-life.org

National Youth Leadership Council
1910 West County Road B
St. Paul, MN 55113-1337
(612) 631-3672 / (612) 631-2955 (fax)
http://www.nylc.org

Youth Service America
1101 15th Street, Suite 200
Washington, DC 20005
(202) 296-2992 / (202) 296-4030 (fax)
http://www.ysa.org

EDUCATION ASSOCIATIONS SUPPORTING CHARACTER EDUCATION

American Association of Colleges of Teacher Education
1307 New York Ave., N.W., Suite 300
Washington, DC 20005-4701
(202) 293-2450 / (202) 457-8095 (fax)
http://www.aacte.org

American Association of School Administrators
1801 N. Moore Street
Arlington, VA 22209-9988
(703) 528-0700 / (703) 841-1543
http://www.aasa.org

American Federation of Teachers
555 New Jersey Ave., NW
Washington, DC 20001
(202) 379-4400
http://www.aft.org

Association for Moral Education
Dr. Darcia Narvaez, Secretary
College of Education and Human Development
University of Minnesota
206 Burton Hall—178 Pillsbury Drive SE
Minneapolis, MN 55455
http://www4.wittenberg.edu/ame/index.html

Association for Supervision and Curriculum Development
1703 North Beauregard Street
Alexandria, VA 22311-1714
(800) 933-ASCD / (703) 575-5400 (fax)
http://www.ascd.org

Association of Teacher Educators
1900 Association Drive, Suite ATE
Reston, VA 20191-1502
(703) 620-3110 / (703) 620-9530 (fax)
http://www.siu.edu/departments/coe/ate/

National Association of Secondary School Principals
1904 Association Drive
Reston, VA 20191-1537
(800) 860-0200 / (703) 476-5432 (fax)
http://www.nassp.org

National Education Association
1201 Sixteenth Street, NW, Suite 800
Washington, DC 20036
(202) 833-4000
http://www.nea.org

National School Boards Association
1680 Duke Street
Alexandria, VA 22314
(703) 838-6722 / (703) 683-7590 (fax)
http://www.nsba.org

Phi Delta Kappa International
408 N. Union Street, P.O. Box 789
Bloomington, IN 47402-0789
(800) 766-1156 / (812) 339-0018 (fax)
http://www.pdkintl.org

NETWORKS AND COALITIONS

The *Character Counts! Coalition* is a national partnership of organizations and individuals involved in the education, training, or care of youth.

Josephson Institute of Ethics
4640 Admiralty Way, Suite 1001
Marina Del Rey, CA 90292-6610
(310) 306-1868 / (310) 827-1864 (fax)
http://www.josephsoninstitute.org

The Character Education Network of the Association of Supervision and Curriculum Development.

Karen Bohlin
Center for the Advancement of Ethics and Character
Boston University
605 Commonwealth Avenue
Boston, MA 02215
(617) 353-3262 / (617) 353-3924 (fax)
http://education.bu.edu/CharacterEd

The *Character Education Partnership* is a nonpartisan coalition of individuals and organizations.

Julea Posey
1600 K Street, NW, Suite 501
Washington, DC 20006
(800) 988-8081 / (202) 296-7779 (fax)
http://www.character.org

References

Association for Supervision and Curriculum Development. (1988). *Moral education in the life of the school.* Alexandria, VA: Author, Panel on Moral Education.

Banas, S. L. (1996). A K–12 story in values education increases awareness in values practices in New York's Sweet Home community. In P. F. Vincent (Ed.), *Promising practices in character education* (pp. 29-40). Chapel Hill, NC: Character Development Group.

Berger, E. (1996). K–12 character education in Locust Valley. *The Fourth and Fifth Rs: Respect and Responsibility, 2*(2), 1-4.

Boyer, E. L. (1995). *The basic school: A community of learners.* Princeton, NJ: Carnegie Foundation for the Advancement of Teaching.

Brooks, B. D., & Goble, F. (1997). *The case for character education.* Northridge, CA: Studio 4 Productions.

California Public Education Partnership. (1996). *Priority one: Schools that work.* Santa Cruz, CA: Center for the Future of Teaching and Learning.

Center for Civic Education. (1995). *The role of civic education: A report of the task force on civic education.* Calabasas, CA: Author.

Chaskin, R. J., & Rauner, D. M. (1995). Youth and caring: An introduction. *Phi Delta Kappan, 76*(9), 670-673.

Child Development Project. (1994). *At home in our schools: A guide to school-wide activities that build community.* Oakland, CA: Developmental Studies Center.

Chrislip, D. D., & Larson, C. (1994). *Collaborative leadership: How citizens and civic leaders can make a difference.* San Francisco: Jossey-Bass.

Davis, K. C. (1990). *Don't know much about history.* New York: Avon.

Delattre, E. J., & Russell, W. E. (1993). Schooling, moral principles, and the formation of character. *Journal of Education, 175*(2), 24-25.

DeRoche, E. F. (1987). *An administrator's guide for evaluating programs and personnel.* Boston: Allyn & Bacon.

DeRoche, E. F. (1999). Character education: A one-act play. *Action in Teacher Education, 20*(4), 100-105.

Dickson, P. (1991). *Timelines.* New York: Addison-Wesley.

Diegmuelier, K. (1996, February 7). AASA reform report urges focus on ethics as schools look to future. *Education Week,* p. 6.

DiGiulio, R. (1995). *Positive classroom management.* Thousand Oaks, CA: Corwin.

Elam, S. M., & Rose, L. C. (1995). The 27th annual Phi Delta Kappan/ Gallup poll of the public's attitudes toward the public schools. *Phi Delta Kappan, 76*(1), 41-56.

Elam, S. M., Rose, L. C., & Gallup, A. M. (1993). The 25th annual Phi Delta Kappan/Gallup poll of the public's attitudes toward the public schools. *Phi Delta Kappan, 73*(1), 137-152.

Elkind, D. (1995). School and family in the postmodern world. *Phi Delta Kappan, 77*(1), 8-14.

Elkind, D., & Sweet, F. (1997, May). The Socratic approach to character education *Educational Leadership, 55,* pp. 56-59.

Epstein, J. L. (1995). School/family/community partnerships: For the children we share. *Phi Delta Kappan, 76*(9), 701-712.

Epstein, J., Coates, L., Salinas, K. C., Sanders, M. G., & Simon, B. S. (1997). *School, family, and community partnerships: Your handbook for action.* Thousand Oaks, CA: Corwin.

Fernald, J. C. (1947). *Standard handbook of synonyms, antonyms, and prepositions.* New York: Funk & Wagnalls.

Frymier, J., Cunningham, L., Duckett, W., Gansneder, B., Link, F. Rimmer, J., & Schulz, J. (1995). *Values on which we agree.* Bloomington, IN: Phi Delta Kappa International.

Frymier, J., Cunningham, L., Duckett, W., Gansneder, B., Link, F., Rimmer, J., & Schulz, J. (1996). Values and the schools: Sixty years ago and now (*Research Bulletin,* Vol. 17, pp. 4-5). Bloomington, IN: Phi Delta Kappa, Center for Evaluation, Development, and Research.

Fullan, M., & Miles, M. (1992). What works and what doesn't. *Phi Delta Kappan, 73*(10), 745-752.

Gardner, H. (1995). *Leading minds.* New York: Basic Books.

Gardner, J. W. (1990). *Reinventing community* (Carnegie Corporation Occasional Papers). New York: Carnegie Corporation of New York.

Gitlin, T. (1987). *The sixties: Years of hope, days of rage.* New York: Bantam.

Goleman, D. (1996). *Emotional intelligence.* New York: Bantam.

Good, T. L., & Brophy, J. E. (1991). *Looking in classrooms* (5th ed.). New York: HarperCollins.

Goodlad, J. (1994). *What schools are for.* Bloomington, IN: Phi Delta Kappa Education Foundation.

Goodlad, J., Soder, R., & Sirotnit, K. (Eds.). (1990). *The moral dimensions of teaching.* San Francisco: Jossey-Bass.

Gordon, T. (1974). *T.E.T.: Teacher Effectiveness Training.* New York: Wyden.

Gursky, D. (1996). Uniform improvement. *Education Digest, 61*(7), 45-48.

Gutmann, A. (1987). *Democratic education.* Princeton, NJ: Princeton University Press.

Hamburg, D. A. (1986). *Preparing for life: The critical transition of adolescence.* New York: Carnegie Corporation of New York.

Hamburg, D. A. (1991). *The family crucible and healthy child development.* New York: Carnegie Corporation of New York.

Hamburg, D. A. (1994). *Education for conflict resolution.* New York: Carnegie Corporation of New York.

Heath, D. (1994). *Schools of hope: Developing minds and character in today's youth.* San Francisco: Jossey-Bass.

Henderson, A. T., & Berla, N. (1994). *A new generation of evidence: The family is critical to student achievement.* Columbia, MD: National Committee for Citizens in Education.

History—Social Science Curriculum Framework and Criteria Committee. (1988). *History—Social science framework for California public schools kindergarten through grade twelve.* Sacramento: California Department of Education.

Hollifield, J. (Ed.). (1995). Schools, families, and students get stronger when parents and teachers take collaboration into their own hands. In *Research and development report* (Vol. 6, No. 5). Baltimore, MD: Johns Hopkins University, Center on Families, Communities, Schools & Children's Learning.

Huffman, H. A. (1994). *Developing a character education program: One school district's experience.* Alexandria, VA: Association for Supervision and Curriculum Development.

Jarvis, F. W. (1993). Beyond ethics. *Journal of Education, 175*(2), 65-66.

Johnson, D. W., Johnson, R. T., Holubec, E. J., & Roy, P. (1984). *Circles of learning: Cooperation in the classroom.* Alexandria, VA: Association for Supervision and Curriculum Development.

Johnson, J., & Immerwahr, J. (1994). *First things first: What Americans expect from the public schools.* New York: Public Agenda.

Kilpatrick, W. K. (1992). *Why Johnny can't tell right from wrong.* New York: Simon & Schuster.

Kirschenbaum, H. (1992). A comprehensive model for values education and moral education. *Phi Delta Kappan, 73*(10), 771-776.

Kirschenbaum, H. (1995). *100 ways to enhance values and morality in school and youth settings.* Boston: Allyn & Bacon.

Kohlberg, L. (1976). Moral stages and moralization: The cognitive-developmental approach. In T. Lickona (Ed.), *Moral development and behavior* (pp. 31-53). New York: Rinehart & Winston.

Kohlberg, L. (1981). *The philosophy of moral development: Moral stages and the idea of justice.* San Francisco: Harper & Row.

Kohn, A. (1991). Caring kids: The role of the schools. *Phi Delta Kappan, 72*(7), 495-506.

Lantieri, L. (1995). Waging peace in our schools: Beginning with the children. *Phi Delta Kappan, 76*(5), 386-388.

Leitman, R. (1996). *Students voice their opinion on learning about values and principles in school.* New York: Metropolitan Life Insurance Company.

Leming, J. S. (1993a). *Character education: Lessons from the past, models for the future.* Camden, ME: Institute for Global Ethics.

Leming, J. S. (1993b). Synthesis of research: In search of effective character education. *Educational Leadership, 51*(3), 63-71.

Leming, J. S. (1998). *Final report: An evaluation of the Heartwood Institute's "An ethics curriculum for children."* Pittsburgh, PA: The Heartwood Institute.

Lewis, C., Schaps, E., & Watson, M. (1995). Beyond the pendulum: Creating challenging and caring schools. *Phi Delta Kappan, 76*(7), 547-554.

Lickona, T. (1991). *Educating for character: How schools can teach respect and responsibility.* New York: Bantam.

Lickona, T., Schaps, E., & Lewis, C. (1996). *Eleven principles of effective character education.* Alexandria, VA: The Character Education Partnership.

Mahaffey, R. (1999). Humanize education for the biotech century. *Education Digest, 65*(4), 4-10.

Medlock, A. (1995, June 21). The ultimate character education: Bringing back heroes. *Education Week, 25,* 43.

Million, J. (1996). Do clothes make the students? *NAESP Communicator, 19*(8), 5.

Moody, B., & McKay, L. (1993). PREP: A process, not a recipe. *Educational Leadership, 51*(3), 28-30.

Murphy, M. (1998). *Character education in America's blue ribbon schools.* Lancaster, PA: Technomic.

National Association of Secondary School Principals (NASSP). (1996). *Breaking ranks: Changing an American institution* (Report of the National Association of Secondary School Principals). Reston, VA: Author.

National Commission on Excellence in Education (NCEA). (1983). *A nation at risk: The imperative educational reform.* Washington, DC: Government Printing Office.

National Commission on the Moral and Ethical Dimensions of Teaching. (1996). *Character education and teacher education.* Unpublished manuscript.

National School Boards Association (1987). *Building character in the public schools: Strategies for success.* Alexandria, VA: Author.

Network for Educational Development. (1994). *Personal responsibility education process (PREP).* St. Louis, MO: Author.

Noddings, N. (1995). A morally defensible mission for schools in the 21st century. *Phi Delta Kappan, 76*(5), 366.

Nucci, L. (Ed.). (1989). *Moral development and character education: A dialogue.* Berkeley, CA: McCutchan.

Orosz, J. J. (1995). The new faces of philanthropy. *International Journal of the W. K. Kellogg Foundation, 6*(2), 4-9.

Pangrazi, R. P., & Dauer, V. P. (1995). *Dynamic physical education for elementary school children* (11th ed.). Boston: Allyn & Bacon.

Parsons, C. (1996). *Serving to learn, learning to serve.* Thousand Oaks, CA: Corwin.

Poplin, M., & Weeres, J. (1992). *Voices from the inside: A report on schooling from inside the classroom.* Pomona, CA: The Claremont Graduate School, The Institute for Education in Transformation.

Ryan, K. (1986). The new moral education. *Phi Delta Kappan, 68*(4), 228-233.

Ryan, K., & Bohlin, K. (1996). *The character education manifesto.* Boston: The Boston University Center for the Advancement of Ethics and Character.

Ryan, K., & Bohlin, K. (1999). *Building character in schools.* San Francisco: Jossey-Bass.

Schaps, E. (1999). The Child Development Project. *Principal, 79*(1), 29-31.

Schaps, E., Lewis, C., & Watson, M. (1996). Classroom community: The missing element in elementary school reform. *Principal, 76*(2), 9-31.

Schaps, E., Watson, M., & Lewis, C. (1996). A sense of community is key to effectiveness in fostering character education. *Journal of Staff Development, 17*(2), 42-47.

Schools of character. (1998). New York: McGraw-Hill.

Schurr, S. L. (1992). *How to evaluate your middle school: A practitioner's guide for an informal program evaluation.* Columbus, OH: National Middle School Association.

Shore, R. M. (1996). Personalization: Working to curb violence in an American high school. *Phi Delta Kappan, 77*(5), 362-363.

Sizer, T. R., & Sizer, N. F. (1999). *The students are watching: Schools and the moral contract.* Boston: Beacon.

Solomon, Z. P. (1991). California's policy on parental involvement: State leadership for local initiatives. *Phi Delta Kappan, 72*(5), 359-362.

Spears, L. (1998). Creating caring leadership for the 21st century. *Not-For-Profit Monthly Newsletter, 5*(9), 2.

Starratt, R. J. (1996). *Transforming educational administration: Meaning, community, and excellence.* New York: McGraw-Hill.

Stratton, J. (1995). *How students have changed: A call to action for our children's future.* Arlington, VA: American Association of School Administrators.

Swap, S. (1993). *Developing home-school partnerships: From concepts to practice.* New York: Teachers College Press.

Task Force on Values Education and Ethical Behavior. (1991). *How to establish a values education program in your school.* Towson, MD: Baltimore County School District.

Thomas, R. S. (1991). Assessing character education: Paradigms, problems, and potentials. *The Clearing House, 65*(1), 52-53.

Tom, A. R. (1984). *Teaching as a moral craft.* New York: Longman.

U.S. Department of Education. (1995). *Riley sends guidelines on religion and schools.* (News Release)

U.S. Department of Education Safe and Drug Free Schools Office. (1996). *Manual on school uniforms.* Washington, DC: Author.

Vessels, G. (1998). *Character and community development: A school planning and teacher training handbook.* Westport, CT: Praeger.

Viadero, D. (1994, October 24). Learning to care: The child development project takes aim at children's intellectual, social- and ethical-development. *Education Week, 14*(8), pp. 31-33.

Vincent, P. F. (1996a). *Developing character in students.* Chapel Hill, NC: View Publications.

Vincent, P. F. (1996b). *Promising practices in character education.* Chapel Hill, NC: Character Development Group.

Weinstein, C. S. (1996). *Secondary classroom management: Lessons from research and practice.* New York: McGraw-Hill.

Williams, M. (1992). *How a value is treated in middle schools: The early adolescent's perspective* (Vols. 1 & 2). Ann Arbor, MI: University Microfilms International.

Williams, M. (1993). Actions speak louder than words: How students view character education. *Educational Leadership, 51*(3), 22-23.

Wynne, E. A. (1988). Looking at good schools. In K. Ryan & J. Cooper (Eds.), *Kaleidoscope: Readings in education* (pp. 201-209). Boston: Houghton Mifflin.

Wynne, E. A., & Ryan, K. (1997). *Reclaiming our schools: A handbook on teaching character, academics, and discipline* (2nd ed.). New York: Macmillan.

Yankelovich, D. (1995, Fall). Three destructive trends. *Kettering Review* (pp. 6-15). Dayton, OH: Charles F. Kettering Foundation.

Index

CORWIN
PRESS

The Corwin Press logo—a raven striding across an open book—represents the happy union of courage and learning. We are a professional-level publisher of books and journals for K–12 educators, and we are committed to creating and providing resources that embody these qualities. Corwin's motto is "Success for All Learners."